Drawing Close
to the Holy Spirit

Also by Sr. Mary Ann Fatula, O.P.,
from Sophia Institute Press:

Heaven's Splendor
And the Riches That Await You There

Sr. Mary Ann Fatula, O.P.

Drawing Close to the Holy Spirit

Keys to a Transformed Life and Joyful Heart

SOPHIA INSTITUTE PRESS
Manchester, New Hampshire

Sophia Institute Press
Box 5284, Manchester, NH 03108
1-800-888-9344

www.SophiaInstitute.com

Sophia Institute Press® is a registered trademark of Sophia Institute.

paperback ISBN 978-1-64413-506-8

ebook ISBN 978-1-64413-507-5

Library of Congress Control Number: 2021936822

First printing

For the glory of the Blessed Trinity

Contents

Drawing Close
to the Holy Spirit

Introduction

What a marvelous difference it makes in our lives when we draw close to the Holy Spirit! Regardless of what our past has been, in every trial or difficulty that may afflict us now, in our every sorrow and joy, when we draw near to the Holy Spirit, our lives change for the better. If we ask the Holy Spirit to help us and to anoint every aspect of our lives, we will see how our days start to flow along more "happily, serenely, and full of consolation." Intimacy with the Holy Spirit is the "secret" of holiness, and of true happiness.[1]

This is not because the Holy Spirit is greater than the Father and the Son, for the Three Divine Persons are the one, same, infinite God. In giving glory to the Holy Spirit, we also glorify the Father and the Son, and in drawing close to the Holy Spirit, we also deepen our intimacy with Them, for the Holy Spirit is Their living Bond of Love.[2] Indeed, it is only after we have grown to know and love the Lord Jesus and His Father that many of us start to desire a deeper closeness with the Holy Spirit. What we may not realize, however, is that intimacy with the Lord Jesus and His Father is given to us through Their beloved Holy Spirit, the "Giver" of life

---

[1] "Cardinal Mercier's Secret of Sanctity," Vultus Christi, May 27, 2009, https://vultuschristi.org/index.php/2009/05/the-cardinals -secret-of-sancti/.

[2] St. Augustine, *On the Trinity* 15.17.27.

to us (see John 6:63). St. Paul assures us that we are unable even to confess that "Jesus is Lord" except by the Holy Spirit (1 Cor. 12:3), the Spirit of the Son who also cries out within us, "Abba, Father" (Gal. 4:6). Every magnificent gift of the Father is brought to us through the redeeming work of His Son and is bestowed on us by Their most tender Holy Spirit, through whom "every blessing is showered upon us, both in this world and in the world to come."[3]

It is wonderfully fitting that, in the Trinity's beautiful plan of love for us, the Third Divine Person, who "completes" the Trinity, is the One who completes, perfects, and distributes every grace and blessing to us.[4] This is why closeness with the Holy Spirit is not an optional devotion added to our life as Christians. Intimacy with the Holy Spirit is at the very core of our Christian life (Gal. 5:25) and is the blossoming within us of the most profound graces of our Baptism and Confirmation.

Through the sacrament of Baptism, the Holy Spirit fills us with the grace by which all three Divine Persons of the Trinity make Their beloved home within us (John 14:23; 1 Cor. 3:16). Confirmation, the "completion" of Baptism, then intimately "seals" us with the Holy Spirit (Eph. 1:13) so that we belong irrevocably to Him and share in the tender "familiarity" with the Holy Spirit that the apostles treasured after Pentecost.[5] And, just as intimacy with the Holy Spirit inflamed the apostles' zeal in proclaiming the risen Lord, it fills us also with a peace and joy that cannot help attracting others to the Lord.

In the following pages, we will meditate on this wonderful gift of drawing close to the Holy Spirit and on the great blessings that

---

[3] St. Basil the Great, *On the Holy Spirit* 15.36.
[4] Ibid., 16.38, 39; St. Gregory of Nyssa, *On "Not Three Gods."*
[5] St. Thomas Aquinas, *Commentary on John* 14, lecture 4, no. 1920.

are ours through intimate friendship with Him. In the first chapter, we will reflect on the gift of drawing near to the Holy Spirit, who powerfully and tenderly transforms our lives with His love and peace and joy. We will meditate next on the precious grace of loving the Holy Spirit, the Father and Son's living Bond of Love and the beloved Friend of our souls. In the third chapter, we will consider how the prayer that the Holy Spirit inspires within us deepens our intimacy with the Holy Spirit and inseparably also with the Father and the Son. We will then reflect on the Holy Spirit dwelling in us as our Healer and Consoler, strengthening and guiding us at every moment of our lives. In the fifth and final chapter, we will meditate on the wonders of our Baptism and Confirmation, whose intimate graces are an indispensable means of our growing close to the Holy Spirit.

The insights in this small book are drawn from saints whose secret of holiness and happiness was their own intimacy with the Holy Spirit. May these saints, our brothers and sisters in the Lord, help us to realize that the same "mighty Champion" who was victorious in them also wants to fill *us* with His transforming love and joy (Rom. 5:5; Gal. 5:22–23). St. Cyril of Jerusalem assures us that at every moment of our lives, the Holy Spirit, our gentle "Protector" and "true Guardian," loves us tenderly and "fights" powerfully for us. Most of all, the Holy Spirit offers every one of us the infinitely precious gift of *Himself*. "Only let us open to Him our doors!"[6] May we open our hearts to the Holy Spirit's intimate love for *us* and experience for ourselves the wondrous difference the Holy Spirit makes in the lives of those who draw close to Him.

[6] St. Cyril of Jerusalem, *Catechetical Lectures* 16.19, 16, 20.

1

The Gift of Intimacy
with the Holy Spirit

⚜

A Transformed Life and a Contented Heart

Closeness with the Holy Spirit: if this wonderful thought attracts our hearts, it is not because *we* are seeking the Holy Spirit. The Holy Spirit is the One who is drawing *us* close.[7] And what happiness this grace brings to our souls! St. Paul tells us that, without the Holy Spirit, our lives are plagued by discontent and destructive habits. When we draw near to the Holy Spirit, however, charity, peace, and joy fill our souls (Gal. 5:19–23). By our own experience, we learn that intimacy with the Holy Spirit is the secret of a transformed life and a joyful heart.[8]

St. Augustine tells us that for many years he was full of distress, chained to sin, which gave him no peace. Finally realizing that

---

[7] St. John Henry Newman, *Meditations and Devotions* (London: Longmans, Green, 1916), p. 398.

[8] St. John Henry Newman, "Sermon 19: The Indwelling Spirit," *Plain and Parochial Sermons* (London: Longmans, Green, 1908), vol. 2, p. 230.

he could not set himself free, he began to pray for the grace to be healed. And the Holy Spirit, who inspired his prayer, powerfully answered it.[9] Like Augustine, we, too, are meant to experience the transforming power of the Spirit of Life (Rom. 8:2) in our own hearts. Our weakness and sinfulness, far from being an obstacle to closeness with the Holy Spirit, help to draw us all the nearer to the Divine Person who truly is the "Father of the Poor."[10] In our every difficulty, the Holy Spirit strengthens us with a love that is "gentle" and "fragrant,"[11] drawing us to what is *good*, and filling us with His joy and peace (Gal 5:16; 1 Thess. 1:6; Rom. 15:13; Acts 13:52).

We receive immense encouragement from the saints, who, in their weakness, surrendered themselves to the Holy Spirit's power and love. The Holy Spirit possessed them, and they were completely transformed (1 Sam. 10:6). Cowardly men were turned into apostles willing to die for the Lord, and saints such as Paul were transformed from enemies of Jesus into those passionately in love with Him. When we ask the Holy Spirit to possess *us*, we, too, will experience the immense difference that closeness with the Holy Spirit makes in our lives. Not only in the good times, but also when everything seems to be going wrong, let us give ourselves and all of our problems, all that causes us worry, stress, and anxiety, completely to the Holy Spirit. If we rely not on ourselves but on the Holy Spirit's strength and grace, we, like the saints, will find that wonderful changes that we are

---

[9] St. Augustine, *The Confessions* 8.5.10–12; 8.11.25–27; 8.12.29–30.

[10] Pentecost Sequence, "Veni Sancte Spiritus," prayed after the Second Reading of the Mass for Pentecost.

[11] St. Cyril of Jerusalem, *Catechetical Lectures* 16.16.

powerless to achieve by our own efforts alone, the Holy Spirit will accomplish in us and for us.[12]

Growing to Know and Love the Holy Spirit

The Holy Spirit wants to give us intimacy with Himself, imparting His own strength to us and making our lives new. But how do we draw near so that the Holy Spirit may work these miracles of love in and for us? In his wonderful encyclical on the Holy Spirit, Pope Leo XIII encourages us simply to start *speaking* to the Holy Spirit dwelling within us (1 Cor. 3:16). Closeness to the Holy Spirit is not a reward offered to holy people but rather a healing remedy and precious gift meant for every one of us.[13]

If we feel dissatisfied and are "borne down with trouble," if we long for more joy and peace in our lives, let us ask the Holy Spirit to help us and to draw us close. If we are already blessed to know and love the Holy Spirit, may we draw even closer. Regardless of what our present is like or what our past has been, let us at this very moment "fly" to the Holy Spirit, who is for every one of us "the never-ceasing fount of light, strength, consolation, and holiness."[14]

In our prayer to the Holy Spirit, Pope Leo urges us to use the "sweetest of names," especially those that the Church employs in the beautiful sequence prayed at the Mass for Pentecost. How powerfully we receive the Holy Spirit's comfort and help when we start to pray with tender words like those suggested by the Pentecost Sequence: "*Father of the poor*, help me. *Sweet Guest* of

---

[12] St. Augustine, Letter 130, to Proba, 15:28; St. Cyril of Jerusalem, *Catechetical Lectures* 16.2.

[13] Pope Leo XIII, Encyclical Letter on the Holy Spirit *Divinum Illud Munus* (May 9, 1897), no. 11.

[14] Ibid.

my soul, comfort me. My *Consoler*, heal me and free me. Most Holy Spirit, I love You and give myself completely to You." As Pope Leo assures us, the Holy Spirit is the very Person of Love, and "nothing is more lovable than Love."[15]

Pope Leo encourages us to speak to the Holy Spirit often throughout the day, praying for His help in our every need and for His anointing upon everything we do. Peace starts to fill our soul when we ask the Holy Spirit to free us from sin, to heal our wounds, and to give us His joy. Distress begins to give way to a contented heart as we learn to thank the Holy Spirit for the countless blessings He has given us, often without our even noticing them. Most of all, the Holy Spirit's strong and tender power increasingly fills us when we ask Him every day for the grace to know and love Him more dearly.

How different our lives become when we resolve to begin every day with prayer to the Holy Spirit, imploring Him to anoint our every breath and every second of our lives. St. John Vianney promises us that, if we do this, particularly when we are discouraged or weighed down with problems, the Holy Spirit's gentle power and peace will take hold of our hearts. Comforted in sadness and strengthened in trials, we will start to find "all sorts of happiness" within us. What is not of God will increasingly lose its attraction to us, and our thoughts, desires, words, and deeds will become more *good*. Most of all, we will discover how "beautiful" it is to be "accompanied" at every moment of our lives by the Holy Spirit, who never ceases to protect and care for us.[16]

---

[15] Ibid., nos. 10, 11. See St. Augustine, *On the Trinity* 15.17.24; St. Thomas Aquinas, *Summa Theologiae* I.37.1.

[16] St. John Vianney, *Instructions on the Catechism*, chap. 3, "On the Holy Spirit," Crossroads Initiative. https://www.crossroadsinitiative.com/media/articles/catechetical-instructions/.

If we are hesitant to surrender ourselves completely to the Holy Spirit, let us draw encouragement from saints such as John Henry Newman. As a youth, Newman had sensed that the Holy Spirit wanted to draw him very close to Himself. But Newman resisted. Suspecting that intimate friendship with the Holy Spirit would constrain rather than free him, he tried to put the Holy Spirit out of his mind: "I wished ... to go my own way." The Holy Spirit, however, would not let go of him. Filling him with good thoughts and desires, with peace and joy and strength even in his weakness, the Holy Spirit inspired Newman to pray to Him every day. And, through "infinite compassion" for him, the Holy Spirit began gently and powerfully to take complete and wonderful "possession" of his soul.[17]

In spite of his initial resistance, Newman grew increasingly close to the Holy Spirit and docile to His tender inspirations. Newman was a priest of the Church of England, an honored fellow at Oxford University, and a respected vicar at St. Mary's, where he preached renowned sermons. He became an esteemed leader of the Oxford Movement, seeking to renew Catholic elements in the Anglican faith. His efforts to identify the foundations of the Church of England in the early Church Fathers and councils, however, estranged him from other Anglican clerics and prelates. After intense prayer and study, Newman became convinced that he could no longer adhere to the Anglican Communion, which he had once believed was the true Church of Christ. He resigned as vicar of St. Mary's, and, with the Holy Spirit's grace and strength, eventually entered into full communion with the Catholic Church.

[17] St. John Henry Newman, *Meditations and Devotions*, pp. 398, 399, 401.

This life-changing decision cost him dearly, as loved family, friends, and colleagues criticized and abandoned him. But the Holy Spirit did not abandon him. Two years after his conversion, Newman was ordained a Catholic priest. His life as a priest and scholar in the Catholic Church brought its own trials, including disappointing outcomes in several ministries, as well as suspicion and prejudice from some members of the Catholic clergy. With time, however, Newman's theological contributions gained the respect they deserved, and Pope Leo XIII honored him by naming him a cardinal of the Church.

In his daily *Meditations and Devotions*, published after his death in 1890, we have a privileged glimpse into Newman's intimacy with and total dependence on the Holy Spirit during his life. Shortly after his conversion to the Catholic Faith, the Holy Spirit had inspired Newman to join and then to establish in England the Congregation of the Oratory, whose founder, St. Philip Neri, was known for his joy and great love for the Holy Spirit. As Newman's own intimacy with the Holy Spirit deepened, his constant prayer to St. Philip was that he, too, would be filled with the same "true devotion" to the Holy Spirit that St. Philip cherished. As Newman notes, it was precisely St. Philip's love for the Holy Spirit that had attracted Newman to this joyful saint.[18]

As we read Newman's *Meditations and Devotions*, we are moved by his confession of complete helplessness without the Holy Spirit's strength and grace. In one of his prayers, he cries out to the Holy Spirit in words that cannot help evoking the same sentiments from our own hearts:

[18] Ibid., p. 278.

I cannot have one good thought or do one good act without Thee. I know, that if I attempt anything good in my own strength, I shall to a certainty fail. I have bitter experience of this.... Lead me forward from strength to strength, gently, sweetly, tenderly, lovingly, powerfully, remembering my ... feebleness, till Thou bringest me into Thy heaven.[19]

Newman also pours out his heart's gratitude to the Holy Spirit for His tender love and "infinite compassion" throughout his life, and especially for the profound grace of drawing him to the Catholic Church: "There were many men far better than I by nature.... Yet Thou, in Thy inscrutable love for me, hast chosen me and brought me into Thy fold.... I did everything to thwart Thy purpose. I owe all to Thy grace."[20]

In a sermon Newman had preached for the feast of Pentecost while he was still a priest of the Church of England, he speaks about the special "comfortings" the Holy Spirit gives to those who are suffering troubles and misfortune. Newman surely is alluding to his own trials, but he is also speaking to every one of us. He reminds us of what we, too, discover by our own experience: without the Holy Spirit, we fail miserably. Focused on ourselves and relying on our own supposed strength, we are filled with anxiety; allured by superficial things, our souls are dissatisfied. When we draw close to the Holy Spirit, however, we begin to experience true peace and tender love, for the Holy Spirit *is* the living Love between the Father and the Son. And, because who "the Holy Spirit is in heaven" He also is "abundantly on earth,"

---

[19] Ibid., p. 398.
[20] Ibid., p. 399.

the Holy Spirit is the "never-failing fount of charity" and of peace and of joy within *us*.[21]

As Newman meditated on the precious graces that the Holy Spirit had so tenderly lavished on him throughout his life, he could only cry out in gratitude, "O Source of my Bliss," "I ... bow down in awe before the depths of Thy love."[22] "Source of my Bliss": what a beautiful name by which to draw close to the Holy Spirit! If, like Newman, we daily beg the Holy Spirit for the grace to know and love Him more dearly, we, too, will be filled with gratitude for the "infinite preciousness"[23] of the Holy Spirit's intimate love for *us*. As Newman himself assures us, where the Holy Spirit is known and loved, doubt, gloom, and dissatisfaction are driven out, and a loving heart and contented spirit enter in.[24]

St. Angela of Foligno is another saint who encourages us to believe how dearly and personally the Holy Spirit loves us and wants to be close to us. On a pilgrimage, Angela had prayed to St. Francis, asking for his help to love the Lord Jesus more deeply and to live her Franciscan life more fervently. In answer to her prayer, Angela was astonished to find that it was not Francis but the *Holy Spirit* who spoke to her heart, telling her of *His* infinite love for and delight in her. Angela was deeply moved to hear the Holy Spirit speak these tender words to her soul: "*Love* me, because you are very much loved by me, much more than

---

[21] St. John Henry Newman, "The Indwelling Spirit," pp. 226, 229, 230.

[22] St. John Henry Newman, *Meditations and Devotions*, pp. 399, 400.

[23] St. John Henry Newman, "The Indwelling Spirit," pp. 224, 228, 226.

[24] Ibid., p. 230.

you could love me."[25] What an exquisite pledge of love; what a tender request for the return of that love! May the Holy Spirit's beautiful words to Angela be seared into our own souls, for the Holy Spirit speaks them to each one of *us*. May we respond with all of our hearts: "Most sweet Holy Spirit, I *do* love You. Please give me the grace to love You more and more dearly. I give myself to You. Possess me completely and make me Your own." At this very moment, let us also ask the Holy Spirit for the grace to begin every day with prayer to Him, prayer to love Him more dearly and to live each day in His intimate presence, filled with His strength, peace, and joy.

Many of us already have experienced wonderful blessings of the Holy Spirit's intimate love for us, even if we have not always realized that the Holy Spirit is the One who has so tenderly imparted them to us. Let us pray for the grace to realize and appreciate now the countless gifts that, in the Trinity's plan of love, the Holy Spirit has brought to us:[26] the joys of loving and being loved; the blessings of a cherished family and good health; the treasure of our gifts and accomplishments; the granting of longed-for healings and favors; the surprise of unexpected blessings; the miracles of wonderful conversions and lives changed for the good; the joy of knowing and loving the Trinity; the gift of cherishing the Mass and the precious sacrament of the Eucharist; the treasured strength and comfort of our Faith.

Whether we have been converted by the Holy Spirit's grace, like St. Augustine of Hippo, or preserved by that same grace, like

---

[25] St. Angela of Foligno, *The Book of the Blessed Angela of Foligno: The Memorial*, in *Angela of Foligno: Complete Works*, trans. Paul Lachance, O.F.M. (New York: Paulist Press, 1993), sect. 3; pp. 139, 140, 141.

[26] St. Basil the Great, *On the Holy Spirit* 15.36.

St. Thérèse of Lisieux, what the Holy Spirit desires from us in return for the manifold blessings He has bestowed on us is simply *our* love, not for His benefit but for ours. The Holy Spirit desires *our* love! Surely, love *is* the easiest and sweetest gift we can give to the Holy Spirit, for "everyone can love."[27] What peace and joy will fill us if we begin each day with a prayer such as this:

> Most sweet Holy Spirit, thank You for loving me so tenderly and faithfully, even when I have not realized or appreciated Your love for me. Thank You for the countless blessings You have given me, even when I have not acknowledged or appreciated them or recognized that it was You who gave them to me. Beloved of my soul, I love You and give myself completely to You. Father of the Poor, help me by Your grace. Anoint my every breath and every second of my life, and possess me completely. Heal me, free me, and fill me with Your love, Your peace, Your joy. Draw me close to Yourself, for I belong completely to You.

The Holy Spirit Teaching, Guiding, and Strengthening Us

In the Pentecost Sequence, we beg the Holy Spirit: "O most Blessed Light divine, shine within these hearts of *Thine* and our inmost being fill." What a beautiful prayer, proclaiming this profound truth of our Baptism and Confirmation: we *belong* to the Holy Spirit, who constantly cares for us, teaching and guiding us by His love. St. Augustine tells us that even when human persons are not present to counsel us, the Holy Spirit is

---

[27] St. Angela of Foligno, *The Book of the Blessed Angela of Foligno: The Memorial*, sect. 4; p. 153.

our beloved Helper and Guide, our inner Teacher (John 14:26) who never leaves us.[28]

As we grow to love the Holy Spirit more dearly, we cannot help becoming more receptive to His inspirations and invitations of love. Our desires deepen to receive the sacrament of Penance, to attend Mass more frequently and devoutly, and to receive the Lord in the Eucharist more lovingly. We are drawn to pray more, to read Scripture, to study the beautiful teachings of the Church, and to learn more about our Faith. We may be inspired to learn about the Holy Spirit by reading the Acts of the Apostles, the epistles of St. Paul, and the Gospels of St. Luke and St. John. Our love deepens for the Blessed Trinity, for the beauty of the Mass, and for the mystery of the Eucharist.

We begin to "see" more deeply the wonders of our Baptism and Confirmation, the mercy given to us in the sacraments of Penance and Anointing of the Sick and the beautiful sacraments of Marriage and Ordination. Our desire grows to do something good with our lives, to have more love in our hearts for those close to us and for those who are in need. We find that we are looking for ways to be more helpful to others, to be of service, especially in our Church community. And a place within us realizes that we are not gaining these insights or growing in these good desires simply through our own efforts. The Holy Spirit, who opens our minds and hearts to what is from God, is tenderly teaching and guiding us "into all truth" (1 Cor. 2:11; John 14:26; 16:13).

St. Basil the Great uses the example of a darkened room that is suddenly flooded with sunshine. In a room without light, we

---

[28] St. Augustine of Hippo, Sermon 293, Office of Readings, feast of St. John the Baptist.

cannot see the true value of things; we could trample on gold and not know it. When sunshine fills the room, however, we begin to see what is precious within it. This experience helps us to understand how intimacy with the Holy Spirit gives us an inner "light," enabling us through love to "see" and appreciate more and more deeply the mysteries of our Faith.[29] As we learn by experience, it is love that enables us truly to know someone dear to us, love that enables us to "see" the heart of our beloved. So, too, the Holy Spirit, the very Bond of Love between the Father and the Son, is the living "Light" in our souls, teaching us through love to know and savor more deeply the things of God.[30]

In so many ways, we experience the Holy Spirit opening to us the treasures of the Church's teachings, enlightening us about the mysteries of our Faith and the beauty and meaning of our own lives and vocations. As we are reading Scripture, we may receive from the Holy Spirit the unexpected gift of a beautiful insight into a truth we have believed but perhaps never have truly appreciated. This may happen during Mass or after we have received the Lord in Holy Communion. We may be spending time in adoration before the Lord in the Blessed Sacrament, or reading a saint's writing, or praying quietly, and suddenly we "see" and are deeply touched by the beauty of the Lord's presence in the Eucharist, the profound meaning of the Mass, or another mystery of our Faith. We may not be able to put our new understanding into words, but it fills our soul with warmth and joy. Sometimes tears flow down our cheeks, especially at Mass, and we can't explain why. These are not tears of

---

[29] St. Basil, *On the Holy Spirit*, 16.38.
[30] St. Cyril of Jerusalem, *Catechetical Lectures*, 16.16.

sadness. They are tears of a heart deeply touched by the Holy Spirit's tenderness.

Again, perhaps at challenging times in which we are anxious and unsure about a decision we need to make, we receive a peace and clarity and joy about what the Lord is calling us to do. Or, when we have to confront difficult situations or hostile persons, we respond with a strength and integrity that we know are not our own. At other times, we may accomplish demanding responsibilities with such ease and so few problems that we *know* that our success is not due to simply our own efforts.

In experiences such as these we learn how intimately the Holy Spirit, who loves us, is also constantly teaching, guiding, and strengthening us, especially through His beautiful seven gifts. These are supernatural habits that the Holy Spirit lovingly imparts to us at our Baptism and deepens in us at our Confirmation. By means of these gifts, the Holy Spirit Himself is gently at work within us, disposing us to follow His inspirations with growing ease and joy.[31]

How wonderfully the Holy Spirit helps us by means of these supernatural gifts! Through wisdom, the greatest of the seven gifts, the Holy Spirit gives us a growing "familiarity" with the things of God, so that we begin to know not simply *about* the Divine Persons of the Trinity, but also truly to *know* each Divine Person, through a love that is tender and intimate. At the same time, we start to "grasp" the truths of our Faith more deeply through a "sweet knowing" that the Holy Spirit of love gives to us.

By means of the gift of understanding, the Holy Spirit gives us an increasingly *intimate* knowledge of the truths of our Faith, so that we seem to pierce to the very heart of what we believe.

---

[31] St. Thomas Aquinas, *Summa Theologiae* I-II.68.1–8.

Through the gift of knowledge, the Holy Spirit deepens our ability to distinguish truth from falsehood about created reality. We appreciate all of creation as the Trinity's gift to us, meant to draw us to the Trinity, but we also realize that nothing created is the answer to our deepest desires. Through the gift of counsel, the Holy Spirit guides us in difficult situations about what we are called to do, giving us insight and clarity about what decisions we need to make.[32]

Through the gift of fortitude, the Holy Spirit fills us with His own power and strength to confront difficult situations, to speak the truth in love, and to do what pleases the Blessed Trinity in challenging circumstances. By means of the gift of piety, the Holy Spirit gives us a tender affection for the Father as our own dear Father, deepening our desire to do good to others as our Father's beloved children. Finally, through the gift of fear of the Lord, the Holy Spirit moderates our desires for pleasure, giving us a distaste for what is not of God and the grace to avoid what does not lead us to God.[33] As these beautiful gifts of the Holy Spirit blossom within us, we increasingly draw what we think, do, and say not simply from ourselves but also, and even more, from the Holy Spirit dwelling intimately within us (Rom. 8:14).[34]

As the Holy Spirit draws us close to Himself, we start to savor in our souls a tender "sweetness" that comes from the Holy Spirit's "sweet-scented" presence within us.[35] In the beautiful Pentecost Sequence, we pray for this very blessing as we glorify the Holy Spirit, our soul's "*Sweet* Guest" and "*Sweet* Refreshment" within

---

[32] Ibid., II-II.45.2; II-II.8.1; II-II.9.1; II-II.52.1–2.

[33] Ibid., II-II.139.1; II-II.121.1; II-II.19. 9.

[34] Ibid., I-II.68.3.

[35] St. Cyril of Jerusalem, *Catechetical Lectures* 16.16.

us. St. Bernard of Clairvaux refers to this "sweetness" when he speaks of the Holy Spirit as the Father's and Son's "utterly sweet" "Kiss." St. John of the Cross and St. John Henry Newman also write lovingly about the intimate "sweetness" of the Holy Spirit in our souls.[36]

This sweetness of the Holy Spirit within us is not weakness. St. Elizabeth Ann Seton referred to the Holy Spirit's sweetness even as she underwent devastating trials. She suffered the heartbreak of her husband's death when she was only twenty-nine years old and was left to provide for her five young children in the midst of financial hardship. Other painful trials afflicted her, including the tragic death of two of her children. And yet, in every trial, Elizabeth relied completely on the intimate guidance, strength, and comfort of the Holy Spirit within her. Elizabeth had been a devout Episcopalian, but the Holy Spirit drew her to the Catholic Church, filling her with love and longing especially for the Lord truly present in the Eucharist. Following the Holy Spirit's inspirations and relying on His tender grace, she became a Catholic. This life-changing decision cost her many of her dearest friends, who turned bitterly against her. Eventually, with resources and strength not her own, she began a school that provided free education to young girls; she also founded the Sisters of Charity of

---

[36] St. Bernard of Clairvaux, *On the Song of Songs*, Sermon 8.1, Hymns and Chants, https://hymnsandchants.com/Texts/Sermons/SongOfSongs/Sermon08/Sermon08.htm; St. John of the Cross, *The Spiritual Canticle* 17.5, 18.6, in *The Collected Works of St. John of the Cross*, trans. Kieran Kavanaugh, O.C.D., and Otilio Rodriguez, O.C.D. (Washington, DC: ICS Publications, 1973), pp. 480, 484; St. John Henry Newman, "The Indwelling Spirit," p. 230.

St. Joseph's, the first congregation of religious sisters established in the United States.

As we read Elizabeth's letters, we are touched not only by her strength and courage but also by the warmth of her mother's heart, and especially by the references she makes to the "sweet" Holy Spirit on whose power she relies. She encourages a Sulpician priest not to be "rough" with her dear son, but rather to be a gentle friend and father, using his authority "with the sweet Spirit of our tender Compassionate Saviour." To Cecilia, her beloved sister-in-law, she writes, "How sweet and peaceful is His Spirit," who anoints us with the "oil of patience and joyful resignation." Sharing the comfort she received from the Holy Spirit in her every trial, Elizabeth assures Cecilia: "How sweetly his Spirit of peace and patience consoles and strengthens his dear children in every situation."[37]

We, too, may have experienced this powerful and tender sweetness of the Holy Spirit, perhaps during Mass or Eucharistic adoration, or while we were praying or reading Scripture, talking with someone about the Lord, or listening to a beautiful hymn or a moving sermon. And we have experienced the difference between what merely human effort produces and what is anointed by the Holy Spirit, between what comes only from human beings and what comes "from God."[38]

We may have felt this difference when we were trying to carry out a major responsibility or task. When we have tried to

---

[37] St. Elizabeth Ann Bayley Seton, Letter 7.147, in *Collected Writings*, ed. Regina Bechtle and Judith Metz (Hyde Park, NY: New City Press, 2002), vol. 2, p. 147; Letters 4.78, 4.76, in *Collected Writings* (Hyde Park, NY: New City Press, 2000), vol. 1, pp. 514, 512.

[38] St. John of the Cross, *The Living Flame of Love* 3.45; p. 627.

accomplish something important without praying first to the Holy Spirit, how often we have faced the inadequacy of merely our own efforts! We may have spent countless hours working on a project, only to see our work bear fruit in a disappointing outcome, or even come to nothing. On the other hand, we may also have received the beautiful grace to cry out to the Holy Spirit in our desperation, "Father of the Poor, Hope of the Hopeless, help me! Most sweet Holy Spirit, Beloved of my soul, I am helpless without You. I give this problem, this situation, this responsibility, this task to You; please *do it for me*. I am Yours; fill me with Your strength and anointing." And then, how different the results! When we ask the Holy Spirit, our "mighty Champion," to work in and through us, He *does* so, not only "powerfully," but also "gently, sweetly, tenderly."[39]

What joy and strength fill our souls as we learn to pray for the Holy Spirit's anointing not only upon our important undertakings but also upon our every breath and upon everything that we think, do, and say. We learn to ask the Holy Spirit especially for the grace always to speak "the truth in love" (Eph. 4:15), particularly when we are called to communicate with an individual or a group or to engage in a conversation that demands from us courage and conviction. If we entrust ourselves to the Holy Spirit, asking *Him* to speak within us and for us, we can trust that we will not be the ones speaking. Rather, as the Lord Himself assures us, the Spirit of our Father will speak powerfully and lovingly through us (Matt. 10:19–20).

When we pray for the Holy Spirit's anointing upon every second of our lives, we discover by experience that everything

---

[39] St. Cyril of Jerusalem, *Catechetical Lectures* 16.16; St. John Henry Newman, *Meditations and Devotions*, p. 398.

the Holy Spirit anoints is beautiful. Even more, we realize with gratitude that intimacy with the Holy Spirit is a grace we could never earn or deserve. Nothing of our own could draw the Holy Spirit to us; only through His infinite love for us has the Holy Spirit drawn near to us. Desiring to fill us at every moment with His own peace and strength and joy, the Holy Spirit has chosen us, weak as we are, and given Himself completely to us. As we meditate on these wondrous blessings, may we respond wholeheartedly to the Holy Spirit's precious gift of Himself to us and give ourselves completely in return.

2

Loving the Person of Love

⚜

Since the wonderful moment of our Baptism, the Holy Spirit has been dwelling within us, loving us and giving Himself to us. How blessed our life becomes when we draw close to the Holy Spirit, responding with all of our love to the Divine Person whose very name is Love.[40]

The Person of Love

"God's love has been poured into our hearts through the Holy Spirit who has been given to us" (Rom. 5:5). As St. Augustine reflected on this beautiful passage from St. Paul, he found in our own experience of love a precious intimation of who the Holy Spirit is at the heart of the Trinity. There is always a "threeness" in our love: we who love, our beloved, and the bond of love between us. In this mystery of created love, Augustine found a tender reflection of the deepest love of all, the Divine Persons' infinite love for one another. As he contemplated the exquisite mystery of the Father's eternal self-giving to His Son, and the Son's ecstatic returning of His Father's love, Augustine was inspired to

---

[40] St. Thomas Aquinas, *Summa Theologiae* I.37.2; I.37.1.

glorify the Holy Spirit as Their infinitely sweet "Embrace," Their exquisite "Delight," Their most intimate Bond of Love.[41]

All three Persons of the Trinity are love by nature, but only the Holy Spirit, the Father's and Son's living Love for one another, is the Divine Person whose distinct personal identity and name are "Love." Even the precious name that we most often use for the Third Divine Person, "Holy Spirit," alludes to this mystery of Love that the Holy Spirit is. The beautiful word *spirit* can mean "breath" or "impulse," and one kind of gentle "breath" is the impulse of love that draws us to our beloved. The Father's and Son's "Impulse of Love" drawing Them eternally to one another, Their mutual "Breath of Love," is the Third Divine Person, the Holy Spirit, whose intimate, personal name is *Love*.[42]

St. Bernard of Clairvaux calls the Holy Spirit not only the Father's and Son's living "Breath of Love," but also Their sweet "Embrace" and tender "Kiss" of Love (Song of Sol. 1:2). The Lord Jesus kissed His apostles with this living "Kiss" when, after His Resurrection, He "breathed" on them His wondrous Holy Spirit (John 20:22).[43] Through the Trinity's intimate love for *us*, we ourselves are blessed beyond all measure to receive the Father's and Son's own "Kiss of Love" at our Baptism, and then to receive the unrestrained fullness of Their eternal, intimate "Kiss" at our Confirmation. Wonderful mystery of love! The Holy Spirit, the Father's and Son's exquisite "Kiss of love," now dwells intimately within *us*, loving us tenderly, delighting in us, and inviting our own response of love in return.

[41] St. Augustine, *On the Trinity* 8.10.14; 6.10.11; 15.17.27.
[42] St. Thomas Aquinas, *Summa Theologiae* I.27.4; I.37.1; I.36.1.
[43] St. Bernard of Clairvaux, *On the Song of Songs* 8.1–2; 8.6–7.

Loving the Person of Love

Our Gift to Possess and Enjoy

We know that love itself is, above all else, a cherished *gift*. When we give our love to someone, we bestow it freely and not because it is owed. When we give a gift to someone dear to us, it is not because it is demanded; in our gift, we are freely giving our *love*. Our experience is a reflection of the exquisite mystery of the Holy Spirit, the Divine Person of Love, whose very name is not only "Love" but also precious "Gift" (Acts 2:38). At our Baptism, all Three Divine Persons give Themselves completely to us as gift so that we may possess Them, enjoy Them, delight in Them. The Holy Spirit, however, is infinite Gift in a unique way. As the Father's and Son's own intimate Love for one another, the Holy Spirit is also *Their* exquisite *Gift* of Love, the living Gift who also gives *Himself* to us, to be truly *ours* to possess and *enjoy* and belong to us forever.[44]

The Holy Spirit gives Himself completely to us, not because we are worthy but because He is the most tender "Father of the Poor."[45] What a consoling name! What gentle miracles of love we experience when we pray to the Holy Spirit using this beautiful, powerful name! In all of our needs, when we feel helpless, when everything seems hopeless, let us cry out to the Holy Spirit, "Father of the Poor, help me!" St. Paul assures us that "God's love has been poured into our hearts through the Holy Spirit," who "has been given to us" (Rom. 5:5). These beautiful words show us how unreserved is the Holy Spirit's self-giving to us who are utterly poor, who have nothing to draw the Holy Spirit's love to us except our helplessness.[46]

---

[44] St. Thomas Aquinas, *Summa Theologiae* I.38.1–2; I. 43.3, 4, 5.
[45] Pentecost Sequence.
[46] St. Thomas Aquinas, *Commentary on John* 3, lecture 6, no. 542.

Drawing Close to the Holy Spirit

The Lord reminds us of how tenderly we ourselves give good gifts to our children, who do absolutely nothing to "deserve" our love. We simply love to give them our love; the more helpless they are, the more we love to help them and give good gifts to them. How much more does our Father in Heaven love to "give the Holy Spirit to those who ask" (Luke 11:13). In our every need, let us simply *ask* the Father to flood our souls with His precious Gift of the Holy Spirit, the Person of Love who is everything good we could want for ourselves and our loved ones. In every situation, when we are happy and when we are troubled, when we are content and when we feel empty and distressed, when our hearts are at peace and when they are broken, let us turn to the Person of *Love*: "Father of the Poor, O Love, Beloved of my soul, give me Your love, Your joy. Satisfy my heart with *Yourself*."

Our Beloved Friend

What is the sweetest, easiest way to grow close to the Holy Spirit? St. Cyril of Jerusalem gives us a beautiful response when he tells us that the Holy Spirit dwells in us with "the tenderness of a true friend."[47] What peace and joy fill our hearts when we learn to speak to the Holy Spirit with the ease and familiarity we show to our dearest Friend! As we begin to *return* the Holy Spirit's self-giving love to us, when we start to *give ourselves* to the Holy Spirit, we savor the happiness not merely of a one-sided love but

---

[47] St. Cyril of Jerusalem, *Catechetical Lectures* 16.16, Office of Readings for Monday of Easter Week Seven, Liturgies.net, http://www.liturgies.net/Liturgies/Catholic/loh/easter/week7 mondayor.htm.

also the tender love that is truly intimate *friendship* with the Holy Spirit, the very Person of Love.

"I do not call you servants any longer ... but I have called you friends, because I have made known to you everything that I have heard from my Father" (John 15:15). The Lord Jesus assures us of His own intimate friendship with us, for He has revealed to us all that His Father has spoken to His heart, and He has given Himself completely to us, sacrificing His life for us (John 15:13, 15). The Holy Spirit, too, however, is our beloved Friend, and in an utterly unique way. Because love is the very heart of true friendship, the Holy Spirit, whose personal name is Love, is, above all, our beloved Friend.[48] A prayer used in the Liturgy of the Hours assures us of this very truth, as we ask the Father to fill us with the same Spirit of Love whom He tenderly gave to the apostles as their own beloved Companion and "constant Friend."[49]

The meditations of St. Thomas Aquinas on the qualities of true friendship help us to appreciate more deeply the beautiful mystery of the Holy Spirit's intimate love for us as our beloved Friend. Thomas tells us, first of all, that true friendship is not a one-sided love; it is the equality and reciprocity of a *self-giving* love that is *mutual* and *good*. We *both* give the gift of ourselves, desiring and working for one another's true good as if it were our very own, loving and helping each other in every way that we can. We share with and listen to one another, delighting in each other's company and taking true joy in each other's accomplishments. As beloved friends, we are a comfort and refuge for each

---

[48] St. Augustine, *On the Trinity* 15.17.29; St. Thomas Aquinas, *Summa Theologiae* I.37.1.

[49] Prayer for Terce, Tuesday of the First Week in Ordinary Time.

other, especially in difficult times. We love to spend time with each other not only when we are happy but also when we are troubled and sad.[50]

Most of all, we want to share all that we have and are with our beloved friend in a true "life together." This does not necessarily mean dwelling together in the same home. On the contrary, people may live under the same roof with another but not have a real "life together" because they never communicate from their hearts with one another. St. Thomas Aquinas stresses that true friendship is based on this intimate, mutual *communication* in which we share with each other our thoughts and desires, our fears and goals, and most of all, all that is in our hearts (John 15:15). Through intimate friendship, we "reveal the secrets" of our heart to one another, as to the "other half of our soul," for we want our beloved friend to know *everything* about us. Realizing that the more we know, the more we love, we desire to understand all that we can about each other, knowing, if possible, even each other's inmost soul.[51]

These beautiful reflections of St. Thomas on true friendship help us to appreciate how intimately the Holy Spirit, the very Person of Love, is our beloved Friend. Since our Baptism, the Father, the Son, and the Holy Spirit have been dwelling in us, loving us unconditionally, giving Themselves to us, and bestowing on us countless blessings. In a most intimate way, however, the Holy Spirit of Love has dwelt in us as our beloved *Friend*, giving Himself unreservedly to us. Imparting to us *His* own joy

---

[50] St. Thomas Aquinas, *Summa Theologiae*, I-II. 28. 1-2; *Summa Contra Gentiles* IV.22.5.
[51] St. Thomas Aquinas, *Commentary on John* 15, lecture 3, no. 2016; *Summa Theologiae* I-II.28.2.

in our trials (Acts 9:31; Rom. 14:17), the Holy Spirit has been protecting us from all that could truly harm us and helping us in our every need.[52]

Even when we have been unaware of His tender presence and unfailing help, the Holy Spirit has spread His sweet "fragrance" within and around us, comforting and healing us, counseling and teaching us, all through love alone. We know how love itself is our teacher when we want to understand more deeply someone dear to us. The Holy Spirit, the very Person of Love, is constantly teaching us, especially through His gift of wisdom (1 Cor. 2:9–13). Giving us insight into the precious mysteries of our Faith, the Holy Spirit opens the eyes of our hearts especially to the beautiful mystery of the Trinity's intimate life of love.[53] Even more, the Holy Spirit enables us tenderly and truly to *love* the Father, the Lord Jesus, and Himself with an unselfish, supernatural love that is the wondrous virtue of charity.

The Holy Spirit's Charity Uniting Us to the Trinity and to One Another

"God's love has been poured into our hearts through the Holy Spirit," who "has been given to us" (Rom. 5:5). In meditating on St. Paul's profound words, St. Thomas Aquinas was inspired to understand that "God's own love" fills us through the beautiful virtue of charity. This exquisite supernatural love is nothing less than an intimate *friendship* with the Trinity and a created sharing in the Holy Spirit. By means of charity, the Holy Spirit unites us to Himself, and to the Father and the Son, whose tender Love He

---

[52] St. Thomas Aquinas, *Summa Contra Gentiles* IV.22.3.
[53] St. Thomas Aquinas, *Summa Theologiae* II-II.45.2.

is,[54] enabling us to love the Trinity *intimately*. What an astounding gift and mystery of love! Through the virtue of charity, our love for the Persons of the Trinity comes not from ourselves (1 John 4:19) but from the Holy Spirit, the very Person of Love!

Without the Holy Spirit's love, we are so wounded by the weakness that is original sin that, in loving, we easily seek our *own* good. The beautiful virtue of the Holy Spirit's charity, however, makes it easy and delightful for us to love the Trinity above all else, with an unselfish *friendship love* that is filled with ease and joy. Through the virtue of charity, the Holy Spirit enables us to delight in Him and in the Father and the Son, not for selfish reasons but because They are infinitely good and immeasurably dear to us.[55]

Nothing gives us more joy than this heavenly virtue of charity, which inseparably unites us also to one another. As St. Thomas Aquinas beautifully comments, when we truly love those dear to us, "for their sake we love all who belong to them." And so it is with our love for the Divine Persons of the Trinity. Through the very same virtue of the Holy Spirit's charity, we love the Trinity and also all those who "belong" to the Trinity.[56]

As we become intimate friends of the Holy Spirit, the Holy Spirit's own love within us conceives in us other wonderful virtues through which we grow in self-giving love not only for the Trinity but also for one another: "Love is patient and kind ... not jealous or boastful," not "arrogant or rude." Love "does not insist on its own way; it is not irritable or resentful" (1 Cor. 13:4–5). How consoling it is to realize that the love that is charity does

54 Ibid., II-II.23.1; II.24.2.
55 Ibid., II-II.23.2; II-II.23.1; II-II. 23.5, ad. 2.
56 Ibid., II-II.25.1; II-II.23.1, ad. 2.

not depend on our feelings but on the Holy Spirit, who permeates our will with His love. Because our love comes from the Holy Spirit of love within us, the closer we draw to the Holy Spirit, the easier and more delightful it is for us to give this love to one another. Even when we feel empty or incapable of loving, the Holy Spirit's charity within us enables us to love others with a love deeper than our own.

The Holy Spirit enables us, first, to love *ourselves* with His love. The Lord Jesus Himself reminds us that we must love others with the love we have for ourselves (Mark 12:31). When our lives are self-centered, when we dislike ourselves and are miserable in our own company, we have no true love for ourselves, and our hearts are empty. Generous, self-giving love overflows from us when our hearts are full, when we are happy and content. The Holy Spirit, the very Person of Love, gives us this contentment. Through the beautiful virtue of charity, we desire and love the *best* good for ourselves, the Blessed Trinity. And because the Holy Spirit enables us to cherish the Trinity dwelling intimately in us as in Their own home (John 14:23), we are truly *happy* in our own company. We take delight in "entering into" our souls, where the Trinity dwell and where we are never alone. Loved tenderly by the very Person of Love, we find *within* us the joy of "good thoughts in the present, the memory of past good, and the hope of future good."[57]

The more intimate our friendship with the Holy Spirit becomes, the more the Holy Spirit's love gives us the contentment and grace to be freed from destructive relationships. Increasingly, we are healed of the need to use or to depend on other human persons for our happiness. Secure and content within ourselves,

[57] Ibid., II-II.25.7.

we grow more loving in our care for one another as members of the Lord's own Body who "belong" to one another: "If one member suffers, all suffer together;" "if one member is honored, all rejoice together" (Rom. 12:5; 1 Cor. 12:12–13, 26).

We want the Holy Spirit of Love to be the very soul of all our relationships. Our love deepens for those dear to us and those who are poor and in need. We find it easier to be more generous with our time, our talents, our resources (1 Cor. 12:4–11). Most of all, we learn that loving with the Holy Spirit's charity is not a matter of feeling but of willing and working for the good of those we are called to love. Every one of us is meant to know the power of the Holy Spirit's love within us to deepen our married love, our love for our spouses, our children, our parents, those dear to us, and all those we are called to help and serve. As the Holy Spirit enlightens us to see more clearly our own faults and weaknesses, we become more compassionate, patient, kind, and generous to one another. In these and so many other beautiful ways, the Holy Spirit blesses us, increasing our desire to glorify the Trinity and to draw others, especially those dear to us, to the Trinity's love.

A beautiful hymn by St. Ambrose implores the Holy Spirit, "Light up our mortal frame, 'til others catch the living flame."[58] With the Holy Spirit's charity taking hold of us, deepening our love for the Trinity and for all those who "belong" to the Trinity, we are inspired to pray with new fervor the Church's wonderful prayer to the Holy Spirit: "Come Holy Spirit, *fill* the hearts of Your faithful and kindle in us the fire of Your love." Yes, most sweet Holy Spirit, *fill* my heart; enkindle in *me* the *fire* of *Your* love!

---

[58] Hymn for Daytime Prayer, Thursday of Week Five in Ordinary Time.

The closer we draw to the Holy Spirit, the Living "Flame of Love," [59] the more the hearts of others are touched and warmed by *His* love within us. The Gospel of John recounts the beautiful story of Mary, the beloved friend of the Lord, whose lavish anointing of the Lord's feet *"filled"* the entire house "with the fragrance of the perfume" (John 12:3). May the home of our own hearts be filled with the warmth and fragrance of the Holy Spirit's love, drawing many others to the wonderful joy of loving the Person of Love.

---

[59] St. John of the Cross, *The Living Flame of Love*, 1.3, p. 540; *Spiritual Canticle*, 17.5, 7, pp. 480, 481.

3

Prayer Inspired by the Holy Spirit

৵

Drawing Close to the Holy Spirit in Prayer

Just as our relationships grow through communication, our intimacy with the Holy Spirit deepens through the loving communication which is prayer. Prayer is so simple, so possible for every one of us because, even "when we do not know how to pray," the Holy Spirit "helps us in our weakness." Regardless of how brief or empty our prayer sometimes may seem to us, the Holy Spirit of Love helps us and intercedes for us "with sighs too deep for words" (Rom. 8:26).

Just as there are different ways of communicating, there are varied forms of beautiful prayer that the Holy Spirit inspires in us: petition and gratitude, praise and worship, adoration and contemplation. The prayer of petition to the Holy Spirit perhaps comes most easily to us, for we are never without the need for something: a longed-for healing or reconciliation; the gift of someone to love; the blessing of a child; the joy of a happy home; a desperately wanted job. We pray for more peace, more love, more joy for ourselves and for those dear to us. Sometimes, in our feelings of emptiness and helplessness, all we can do is cry out, "Most dear Holy Spirit, Hope of the Hopeless, help me."

Drawing Close to the Holy Spirit

Because the Holy Spirit is the One who inspires us to pray, our prayers of petition are always answered, perhaps not always in the way we want, but always in a way that is better than anything we could have wanted. When our petitions *are* granted in the way we desired, when we realize with joy the blessings that we have received in answer to our prayer, the Holy Spirit draws us even closer to Himself by moving us to prayers of heartfelt thanksgiving and gratitude: "Thank You, most sweet Holy Spirit! I give You glory!" "All praise to You, most Blessed Trinity!"

In addition to prayers of petition and gratitude, the Holy Spirit inspires in us also the beautiful prayer that is worship, adoration, and contemplation. We know how much we love simply to "waste time" with those dear to us, enjoying their company and just "being" together. This is how our bonds of love deepen, and this is how our closeness to the Holy Spirit grows: through "wasting time" with the Holy Spirit, resting in His closeness and simply enjoying His most sweet and intimate presence within us.

A wonderful way to become more receptive to this prayer "too deep for words" (Rom. 8:26) is through gently repeating in our hearts brief prayers using one or more of the Holy Spirit's intimate names. How often we ourselves use affectionate names for those close to us, names we may tenderly speak only when we are with our loved ones. Even more does the Holy Spirit, who is the Father and Son's intimate Love, inspire in our hearts tender names by which He wants us to draw near, names full of affection, such as "Joy of my soul," "my Comforter," "Sweet Love," "Father of the Poor," and "Beloved of my soul."

The Church's hymns and prayers to the Holy Spirit are a beautiful help to us in becoming accustomed to this intimate form of prayer. As we have seen, Pope Leo XIII urges us to pray to the Holy Spirit as the Church does, by "calling upon Him by the sweetest of names."[60] The ancient hymn "Come Creator Spirit"[61] suggests to us some of these "sweetest of names," which we can use in prayer that calms our hearts and brings peace to our souls: "Most dear Holy Spirit, my Comforter, heal my heart." "Sweet Love, possess my soul." "Most sweet Holy Spirit, protect me from all evil." "Dear Holy Spirit, fill me with Your love." "Most sweet Holy Spirit, draw me close to the Father and the Lord Jesus."

In one ancient hymn to the Holy Spirit,[62] we adore the living "Fire of Love," who fills the universe and guides the stars, giving light and life to all. This beautiful hymn suggests other precious names for us to use in drawing near to the Holy Spirit in prayer: "Consoler of the Sorrowing, comfort my soul." "Refuge of the Poor, help me." "Help of the Oppressed, I trust in You." "Most sweet Love, forgive my sins and heal my heart." "Dearest Holy Spirit, free me from doubt and fear. Give me confidence and trust in You." "Most sweet Holy Spirit, heal my anxiety." "Dearest Love, I am sad and lonely. Give me Your love and peace and joy."

There is perhaps no more wonderful prayer to the Holy Spirit than the exquisite hymn, "Come, Holy Spirit."[63] Sung as the sequence after the second reading in the Mass for Pentecost,

---

[60] Pope Leo XIII, *Divinum Illud Munus*, no. 11.

[61] "Veni, Creator Spiritus," ninth-century hymn attributed to Rabanus Maurus.

[62] "Qui procedis," twelfth-century hymn to the Holy Spirit attributed to Adam of St. Victor.

[63] "Veni, Sancte Spiritus," the "Golden Sequence," thirteenth-century hymn attributed to Stephen Langton.

this mystical hymn suggests to us still other tender words with which we can pray to the Holy Spirit throughout the day: "'Father of the Poor, help me." "Most sweet Holy Spirit, I love You and give myself to You." "My Consoler, hold me close." "Sweet Guest of my Soul, I adore You." With words full of affection, we may pray, "Most sweet Holy Spirit, melt the hardness of my heart." "O Love, refresh my weary soul." "Dearest Holy Spirit, heal my wounds." "My Teacher, guide my every step." "Hope of the Hopeless, help me." "Sweet Love, give me Your strength and grace." "Beloved Holy Spirit, I love You." "My Comforter, heal my mind and heart." "Most Sweet Holy Spirit, I love and adore You." "O Love, possess my soul."

A beautiful prayer attributed to St. Augustine[64] suggests to us still other tender words we can use in praying to the Holy Spirit throughout the day: "Most dear Holy Spirit, Strength of the Weak, help me." "Support of the Fallen, give me Your grace." "Teacher of the Humble, enlighten me." "Hope of the Afflicted, I trust in You." "Consoler of the Abandoned, I take refuge in You." "Protector of the Needy, all of my hope is in You." "Strength of the Weak, help me." "Lover of the Humble, I worship You." "Hope of the Dying, I trust in You." "Most sweet Holy Spirit, fill me with Your love."

A deeply treasured hymn to the Holy Spirit chanted in the Byzantine Rite offers us still more tender names by which we can speak intimately to the Holy Spirit in prayer:

[64] "Prayer for the Indwelling of the Spirit," attributed to St. Augustine of Hippo, posted on Chosen to Be Catholic, March 4, 2016, https://catholicprayersonline.wordpress.com/2016/03/04/prayer-for-the-indwelling-of-the-spirit-by-st-augustine-of-hippo.

Heavenly King, Comforter, Spirit of Truth, everywhere present and filling all things, Treasury of Blessings and Giver of Life, come and dwell within us, cleanse us of all stain, and save our souls, O Gracious Lord.[65]

Another wonderful hymn to the Holy Spirit, composed by St. Ambrose of Milan, was beautifully translated by St. John Henry Newman.[66] Full of praise and adoration, we beg the Holy Spirit: "Our souls possess with Thy full flood of holiness!" We ask that our entire being, with every one of its powers, may give praise to the Holy Spirit, the Person of Love. With deep affection, we pray, "O Love, light up my mortal frame, 'til others catch the living Flame!" How close our relationship with the Holy Spirit becomes when we pray every day to Him with words such as the ones used in this lovely hymn!

An especially beautiful name for the Holy Spirit is suggested by the tender prayer of Désiré-Joseph Cardinal Mercier:

I am going to reveal to you the secret of sanctity and happiness. Every day ... enter into ... the sanctuary of your baptized soul (which is the temple of the Holy Spirit) and say to Him: "O Holy Spirit, Beloved of my soul, I adore You. Enlighten me, guide me, strengthen me, console me.... I promise to submit myself to all that You desire of me."

---

[65] "Heavenly King, Comforter," Metropolitan Cantor Institute, Byzantine Catholic Archeparchy of Pittsburgh, https://mci.archpitt.org/songs/English/Heavenly_King_Comforter.html.

[66] Hymn for Daytime Prayer, Thursday of Week Five in Ordinary Time.

Mercier promises us, "If you do this, your life will flow along happily, serenely, and full of consolation, even in the midst of trials."[67]

"Beloved of my soul": what a beautiful name for the Holy Spirit! St. Thomas Aquinas tells us that, through sanctifying grace, all Three Divine Persons dwell in us as the "beloved" dwells in the "lover."[68] All the more does the beautiful name "Beloved" belong to the Holy Spirit, the very Person of Love dwelling intimately in our souls. In his magnificent prayer, Mercier uses the exquisite name, "*Soul* of my soul," which itself illumines the precious name often given as its English translation, "*Beloved* of my soul." Our immortal soul is the wondrous, created spiritual source of our life as human persons. We spontaneously express this truth when we tenderly say to someone dear to us, "I love you with all of my *soul*." Truly, our loved one *is* the *beloved* of our *soul*, the beloved of the deepest core of our being, of the inmost center of who we are.

The very source of the *supernatural* life of our soul, however, is the *Holy Spirit* of Love. How truly we cry out to the Holy Spirit, then, "O *Soul* of my soul," "*Beloved* of my soul," "Beloved of the very *core* of who I am!" What peace and strength and consolation fill us when we learn to pray to the Holy Spirit, "Soul of my soul, possess me!" "Beloved of my soul, I love You!" Speaking to the Holy Spirit with tender words such as these soon becomes

---

[67] "Cardinal Mercier's Secret of Sanctity." Désiré-Joseph Cardinal Mercier of Belgium was known internationally for his courage in leading the resistance during the German occupation of Belgium during World War I. Mercier is said to have composed his beautiful prayer on a pilgrimage to Our Lady of Walsingham, England.

[68] St. Thomas Aquinas, *Summa Theologiae* I.43.3.

a habit, calming us when we are worried, giving us peace when we are anxious, filling us with strength when we are helpless. When we feel worried and weighed down with troubles, when we struggle with temptations and doubts and fears, let us give everything to the Holy Spirit of Love, speaking to Him about all that concerns us. If we ask the Holy Spirit to help us, gently repeating the powerful and tender names, "Father of the Poor," "Beloved of my soul," our hearts will be strengthened and made calm by the Holy Spirit's tender peace.

Such prayer throughout the day will inspire us to set aside explicit time for prayer, time simply to rest in the Holy Spirit's presence, savoring His peace in our souls. If we are filled with what seem to be distractions, let us give all that troubles us to the Holy Spirit and gently repeat a brief and tender prayer to the Holy Spirit. St. John Vianney assures us that it is through such prayer that our "troubles melt away" as snow melts in the sun's rays. "Like honey descending into the soul," this kind of gentle, peaceful prayer is "a foretaste of Heaven, an overflow of paradise" that fills our souls with the "sweetness"[69] that is a special fruit of closeness with the Holy Spirit.

The Holy Spirit Deepening Our Intimacy with the Father and the Son

An inseparable effect of closeness with Their most sweet Holy Spirit is a deepening intimacy also with the Father and the Son. Many of us come to know and love each Divine Person of the Trinity at different times in our lives. We may develop first a close

---

[69] St. John Vianney, *Instructions on the Catechism*, chap. 8, "On Prayer."

relationship with the Lord Jesus, our beloved Savior and Spouse, our cherished Lord and Brother. At another time, we may come to know intimately the Father of the Lord Jesus as our very own Father in Him. We know that such intimacy with the Father and the Son is a precious gift to us. What we may not realize is that this closeness is bestowed on us by Them through Their most tender Holy Spirit. We are reminded of this very truth when we pray in the beautiful hymn "Come, Creator Spirit" ("Veni, Creator, Spiritus"), "May Thy grace on us bestow, the Father and the Son to know."

St. Paul assures us that "no one can say 'Jesus is Lord' except by the Holy Spirit" (1 Cor. 12:3), and that only through the Spirit of the Son are we able to cry out, "Abba, Father" (Gal. 4:6; Rom. 8:15). Surely, it is the Lord Jesus who reveals His beloved Father to us, and the Father who reveals His cherished Son to us (Matt. 11:27; Luke 10:22). The grace of *intimately* knowing the Lord Jesus and His Father, however, is a gift we receive through Their most intimate "Kiss" of love, the Holy Spirit.[70] We can know *about* the Father and Son without the Holy Spirit, but mere information is not the kind of knowledge that the Holy Spirit imparts to us. We truly know someone dear to us only through *love*, and we intimately know the Father and the Son only through Their living Love and most sweet Kiss, the Holy Spirit.[71]

As we have seen, St. Bernard of Clairvaux loved to meditate on the exquisite mystery of the Father's eternally giving all that He is to His Beloved Son, "kissing" Him with a "Kiss that is utterly sweet," "utterly a mystery." The Son ceaselessly receives His Father's self-giving and gives Himself unreservedly in return.

[70] St. Bernard of Clairvaux, *On the Song of Songs*, Sermon 8.3; 8.5.
[71] Ibid., 8.5; 8.6.

Their beloved Holy Spirit *is* Their mutual and tender "Embrace" and "Kiss of love," sweeter than all we could imagine. It is a wondrous mystery of the Trinity's love for us that, through the grace of our Baptism, *we* now have dwelling within us, as *our* Beloved, the Father and Son's very own "Kiss of love," the Holy Spirit, who never ceases to draw us close to Them.[72]

The Holy Spirit Drawing Us Close to Jesus in Prayer

A first inseparable blessing of our intimacy with the Holy Spirit is a deeper closeness also with the Lord Jesus. It is the love "poured into our hearts through the Holy Spirit" (Rom. 5:5) that enables us truly to "see" who the Lord Jesus is[73] and to grow in love for Him. Drawing our hearts to the beauty and tenderness of Jesus, the Holy Spirit reveals to us, most of all, the depths of God the Son's infinite love for us. It is His magnificent, immeasurable love for us that impelled Him to become incarnate, to live a life of unreserved self-giving to us, and to hand Himself over to the horrendous suffering of His Passion and death, all for our sake.

St. Bonaventure describes the intimate response that the Holy Spirit inspires in us when we take time simply to gaze at the Lord Jesus on the Cross. As we truly look with love at the Lord on the Cross, His awful and glorious "throne of mercy," the Holy Spirit fills our hearts with "wonder and joy," with love and gratitude, with "praise and jubilation." And when we contemplate the sacred wounds of the Lord, it is the Holy Spirit of Love who enables us to taste the heavenly bliss that the Lord Himself promised to the thief on the cross beside Him: "Today

[72] Ibid., 8.1; 8.6; 8.7.
[73] Ibid., Sermon 8.5; St. Basil the Great, *On the Holy Spirit* 18.46.

you will be with me in Paradise" (Luke 23:43). We, too, are swept up into Paradise when we take time simply to gaze upon the crucified Lord. As we do so, the Holy Spirit imparts to us a sweet and "mystical wisdom" that inflames our inmost souls with love for the Lord Jesus.[74]

The Holy Spirit of love also enables us to "see" more deeply the beauty, power, and meaning of the Lord's glorious Resurrection, Ascension, and outpouring of the Holy Spirit at Pentecost, all for our sake. We grow to realize who we truly are because of these astounding events: cherished brothers and sisters of the Lord Jesus, beloved sons and daughters of His Father.[75] As we see how deeply treasured we are, the Holy Spirit inspires within us prayer to the Lord Jesus that is intimate and loving: "Most Sacred Heart of Jesus, I trust in You." "My Lord Jesus, have mercy on me, a sinner." "Dearest Lord, hide me in Your precious wounds." "Sweet Jesus, bathe me in Your Blood." "My Lord Jesus, I give myself and all of my troubles to You." "Sweet Jesus, I love You."

We may be drawn to sing or say aloud or in our hearts treasured hymns, prayers, and litanies that give us tender words to use as our own in praying to the Lord Jesus. St. Bernard of Clairvaux describes an especially beautiful way in which the Holy Spirit inspires us to draw close to the Lord: simply saying with love the most sacred name of Jesus. What can equal "the power of His name" "to refresh the harassed senses"? If we are feeling sad, the beautiful name of *Jesus* brings to us a "cloudless sky." Have we fallen into sin? Are we brought "to the brink of despair"? Let us "invoke this life-giving name" and our "will to live will

---

[74] St. Bonaventure, *The Journey of the Mind to God*, 7.4, Office of Readings, feast of St. Bonaventure.

[75] St. Gregory of Nyssa, *On the Holy Spirit*.

be at once renewed." The power of the precious name of Jesus "banishes bitterness and softens hearts."[76]

When we are terrified "before impending peril," when we are filled with doubt, discouraged, and "beaten down by afflictions," the saving power of the sweet name of Jesus brings us courage and a renewed will to live. In every distress we may suffer, "this name is medicine," the "healing remedy" for our every ill. St. Bernard urges us to carry the precious name of Jesus in our hearts, "hidden as in a vase." If we do this, the Holy Spirit will enable us, in our every need, to taste in our souls the sweetness of Jesus, who "is honey in the mouth, music in the ear," the "song" in our hearts![77]

As the Holy Spirit deepens our love for the Lord Jesus, He also fills us with growing love and appreciation for the priceless gift of the Mass and for the Lord's intimate presence in the sacrament of the Eucharist. At every Mass, the Lord Jesus Himself makes present to us His saving death and Resurrection, the mystery of His Last Supper, at which He also feeds us with His most precious Body and Blood. The Lord Himself solemnly assures us, "This *is* my *Body*; this *is* my *Blood*" (Mark 14:22, 24). The Holy Spirit enables us to "see" and to savor more and more deeply this astounding mystery of love. In the Eucharist, we truly receive sacramentally the precious Blood and sacred Body of the Lord Jesus, the "body born of the Virgin," "the true flesh" of the Lord crucified for our sake.[78]

Do we wonder why, in response to such a "great grace," the Church urges us not to absent ourselves from these sacred mysteries? Who gives us the faith to "see" and to love the magnificent

---

[76] St. Bernard of Clairvaux, *On the Song of Songs*, Sermon 15.6.

[77] Ibid., 15.6; 15.7.

[78] St. Ambrose of Milan, *On the Mysteries* 9.53.

mystery of the Mass and the exquisite gift of the Lord's own precious Body and Blood in the Eucharist? Who gives us a growing desire to attend Mass more frequently, to receive the Lord more devoutly, to spend more time adoring the Lord in the Blessed Sacrament? Only the Holy Spirit, who inspires within us the tender response of love: "Taste and see that the LORD is good!" (Ps. 34:8).[79]

The Holy Spirit Drawing Us
Close to the Father in Prayer

The Holy Spirit, who enables us to cry out in love, "Lord Jesus" (see 1 Cor. 12:3), also inspires within us intimate prayer to the Father (Rom. 8:15). The Father is tenderly revealed to us by His only begotten Son (John 1:18), in whom we have become the Father's beloved children through grace. To satiate our hearts with the joy of this truth, the Father has sent "the Spirit of his Son into our hearts, crying out, 'Abba! Father!'" (Gal. 4:6). The same Holy Spirit in whom the Lord "rejoiced" (Luke 10:21) fills *us* with love for the Father as our very own Father in Jesus[80] and immerses *us* also in the "immense ocean of tenderness" that is the Father.[81] Wonderful mystery of love! We have not simply a Creator but a tender *Father* to whom we belong. We know who we truly are, and where our treasured *home* is, where we are chosen and infinitely cherished. We have a compassionate Father who infinitely loves us and provides for us as His beloved sons and daughters in Jesus.

[79] Ibid., 9.58.
[80] St. Bernard of Clairvaux, *On the Song of Songs*, Sermon 8.5.
[81] Servant of God Archbishop Luis Martinez, *True Devotion to the Holy Spirit* (Manchester, NH: Sophia Institute Press, 2000), pp. 100, 101, 103.

No one has ever seen the Father, and yet we can "see" our unseen Father in His only Begotten Son, who has become flesh for our sake (John 1:14, 18). When the apostle Philip asked the Lord to *show* him the Father, the Lord responded to Philip and to every one of us: "Whoever has seen *me*, has seen the *Father*" (John 14:9). And what do we "see" about our beloved Father when we look at the Lord Jesus? We see, most of all, the infinite tenderness of our Father for us, reflected in the Lord's own gentle love as He cherishes children, dines with outcasts, heals the sick, and forgives sinners.

It is His *Father's* tenderness that we see mirrored in the Lord, who is "greatly disturbed in spirit and deeply moved" by the weeping of the sisters and friends of Lazarus after his death. The Lord is so moved by love for Lazarus that He Himself *weeps* and then raises him from the dead (John 11:33–35; 43–44). His heart is so deeply touched by the sight of a widow grieving the death of her only son that He raises her son from the dead (Luke 7:12–15).

We gaze on our *Father's* compassion for us mirrored in the Lord Jesus as He gently welcomes the affection of a woman who washes His feet with her tears, wipes them with her hair, and tenderly kisses them (Luke 7:38). And, at His death, the Lord Jesus not only forgives His executioners; He also makes excuses for them: "Father, forgive them; for they do not know what they are doing" (Luke 23:34). What infinite tenderness; what exquisite compassion! As we read these beautiful Gospel accounts, the Holy Spirit touches us, opening the eyes of our hearts to see in the Lord's immense love the infinite tenderness of our beloved *Father* for *us*, His cherished sons and daughters.[82]

[82] Ibid., p. 102.

The Lord Jesus also *speaks* to us about His Father, assuring us, "The Father Himself loves you" (John 16:27). To help us believe this precious truth, the Lord tells us a beautiful parable about a young man who squanders his inheritance and wastes his life on sin. In desperation he decides to return to his father, expecting to be treated only as a hired hand. "But while he was still far off, his father saw him and was filled with compassion; he ran and put his arms around him and kissed him" (Luke 15:20). To his older son's objections, the father tenderly replied, "Son, you are always with me, and all that is mine is yours. But we had to celebrate and rejoice, because this brother of yours was dead and has come to life; he was lost and has been found" (Luke 15:31–32).

We have read or heard this beautiful parable countless times. But when the *Holy Spirit* speaks it to our hearts, we truly *hear* it and are moved by it. The Holy Spirit is the One who enables us to "see" and believe how infinitely *we* are loved by *our Father* and how lavishly He showers every blessing on us, His infinitely treasured children.[83] Our Father loves us so dearly that He has counted every hair on our heads (Matt. 10:29–30), intimately knowing and providing for our every need even before we ask Him (Matt. 6:26, 31–32). The Lord Himself gently assures us, "*Your* Father knows what you need" (Matt. 6:8). There is *nothing* our Father will not give us for our good. Having given us His own beloved Son (John 3:16) to be crucified for our salvation, He also gives *Himself* completely to us and holds nothing else back from us, including His own precious Kiss of Love, the Holy Spirit (Luke 11:13). The Lord Jesus Himself calls the Holy Spirit "the Spirit of *your* Father" (Matt. 10:20). It is His own Spirit of

---

[83]   St. Gregory of Nyssa, *On "Not Three Gods."*

Love who draws us close to the Father, filling us with trust and confidence in Him and inspiring us to cry out in prayer, "My Father, I love You. I trust You to provide for all that my family and I need." "My Father, may Your precious will be perfectly done in me."

It is no wonder that, as we draw near to the Holy Spirit in prayer, our love for our Father and trust in His provident care for us also deepen. How many of us have experienced throughout our lives the wonders, the miracles, of our Father's tender providence for us! As we grow close to the Holy Spirit, we become even more trusting in our Father's love and care and in His providing for our every need. We grow even more peaceful and content with our Father's beautiful plan of love for us and are increasingly freed from anxiety about our needs and from fears about our future.

The Holy Spirit inspires us to cry out in prayer to our beloved Father, "Thank You, dearest Father, for providing so wonderfully for my every need." "My Father, protect me from all harm and hold me close." "Dearest Father, we place all of our hope in You." "My Father, I adore You and love You." "Dearest Father, we trust in Your tender and provident care for us." "Beloved Father, into Your hands, I commend my spirit" (see Luke 23:46).

As the eyes of our hearts are opened to see how merciful our Father has been with *us*, we, too, grow more compassionate, merciful, and forgiving of others (Luke 6:36).[84] When we pray the Our Father, the Holy Spirit enables us to realize more deeply the Father's infinite delight in hearing the precious words of His beloved Son on *our* lips. And the more lovingly we pray the Our Father, the more deeply we are inspired to live the words that

---

[84] St. John Henry Newman, *Sermon* 19; II, pp. 225, 226.

we pray.[85] Because of the Holy Spirit's presence within us, these blessings of intimacy with our Father fill us with a trust and confidence[86] that change our lives and touch the hearts of others.

The Holy Spirit Praying within Us

Growing close to the Holy Spirit, we also begin to savor a peace that draws us simply to rest in the Trinity's loving presence within us. Meditation and reading can help to calm our hearts for this kind of intimate prayer, but the Holy Spirit also may inspire us to put aside our reading and thoughts simply to rest peacefully in the Trinity. In this contemplative prayer, we are drawn to repose in the Father's love, to savor the Holy Spirit's tenderness, and, like the beloved disciple, to rest close to the heart of Jesus (John 13:23).

Initially, the beginning of this quiet prayer may seem to be only dryness and distractions. We may feel that nothing is happening and that we are wasting our time. St. John of the Cross assures us, however, that if we try to meditate or read instead of simply resting peacefully in the Divine Persons' intimate presence, we risk losing the Holy Spirit's "delicate anointings."[87] When we are given this quiet prayer without many words, let us follow the advice of St. Francis de Sales, who urges us to "let go of the reins" and allow the Holy Spirit to pray within us.[88] If we struggle with distractions that seem to prevent us from resting in

---

[85] St. Cyprian, Treatise 4, *On the Lord's Prayer*, 2–3; 11.

[86] Archbishop Luis Martinez, *True Devotion to the Holy Spirit*, p. 101.

[87] St. John of the Cross, *The Living Flame of Love*, 3.43; 3.31; pp. 626, 621.

[88] St. Francis de Sales, *Introduction to the Devout Life* (Grand Rapids, MI: Christian Classics Ethereal Library), chap. 8; p. 60.

this quiet prayer, let us simply speak to the Holy Spirit about our problems and worries and then gently keep repeating invocations such as these: "Most sweet Holy Spirit, help me." "I give all of my troubles to You." "Father of the Poor, calm my heart with Your peace." "Sweet Love, possess me."

Sometimes, when the Holy Spirit inspires in us the prayer of petition or praise, we may run out of words but still want to keep on imploring or praising. Let us then allow the Holy Spirit to pray within us, not with words, but with sounds and syllables that surpass our words. St. Paul himself speaks about "praying in tongues," in which it is not our minds but our spirits that pray (1 Cor. 14:14).

St. Augustine, too, encourages us to pray with "jubilation in the Spirit." If we are unable to express in words our petition or praise, the Holy Spirit may inspire in us the prayer in which our hearts simply "rejoice in a song without words."[89] Inspired by the Holy Spirit, saints such as Romuald would cry out in love and joy, repeating beautiful names for the Lord: "Jesus, beloved, sweet honey … delight of the saints!"[90] St. Thomas Aquinas quotes a wonderful gloss on Psalm 46 (47) describing this prayer of "jubilation" as an "ineffable joy" in God, joyful prayer that "cannot be kept silent" but also cannot be expressed in words because "it exceeds comprehension."[91]

These varying kinds of prayer, inspired by the Holy Spirit within us, help us to form a habit of prayer throughout the day.

---

[89] St. Augustine, *Discourse on the Psalms*, Ps. 32, Office of Readings, feast of St. Cecilia.

[90] St. Peter Damian, *Life of St. Romuald*, Office of Readings, feast of St. Romuald.

[91] St. Thomas Aquinas, *Commentary on Psalm 46*, trans. Steven Loughlin, http://hosted.desales.edu/w4/philtheo/loughlin/ATP/.

Whatever we are doing, we can be humming, singing, or praying in our hearts. The Holy Spirit may inspire us to pray to our Father, to rest in His love, to thank and praise Him for His tender care and providence. At other times, we may be drawn to pray to the Lord Jesus, begging Him to cover us and our loved ones with His most precious Blood, imploring Him to have mercy on us and on the world. We may be inspired to speak tenderly to the Holy Spirit and to enjoy His sweetness within us. In these and so many other beautiful ways, the Holy Spirit fulfills in us the tender exhortation "Pray in the Spirit at all times" (Eph. 6:18).

Living in the Holy Spirit's Presence

For encouragement in living in the Holy Spirit's intimate presence throughout the day, it is difficult to find a more endearing saint to teach and inspire us than St. Catherine of Siena. Her close friend and confessor, Bl. Raymond of Capua, tells us that because she was filled with the "fire of the Holy Spirit" from her youth, she exerted a wonderful influence and "mysterious attraction" on others. Not only her compelling words but also her very presence drove out "despondency from the hearts of any who shared her company." The Holy Spirit's joy within her soul "banished dejection of spirit and all feelings of depression," bringing instead a wonderful peace to anyone near her. "Filled with a joy which they had never felt before," those blessed to be in her presence were inspired to cry out in their hearts: "It is good for us to be here."[92] This beautiful attraction that Catherine

---

[92] Bl. Raymond of Capua, *The Life of Catherine of Siena.* Trans. Conleth Kearns, O.P. (Wilmington, DE: Michael Glazier, 1980), nos. 9, 27; pp. 8, 28.

exerted on others came from the Holy Spirit, the very "source of spiritual joy,"[93] who so wonderfully filled the hearts of the early disciples (Acts 13:52).

Catherine learned to rely completely on the Holy Spirit as her beloved Friend and faithful Teacher. When she was a young woman, Catherine's family determined that she would marry. Filling her day with household chores, they intended to deprive her of time and a place for intimate prayer with the Lord Jesus, the only Spouse she desired. Taught by the Holy Spirit, however, Catherine discovered that "the Kingdom of God" truly is within us (see Luke 17:21). She found in her soul the place of prayer that she would never have to leave. As the Holy Spirit continued to teach and guide her, Catherine learned to entrust herself completely to her beloved "indwelling Guest."[94]

Eventually, Catherine's family relented and allowed her to devote her time to prayer. After several years, the Holy Spirit drew Catherine to a life of service and then to a public life in the Church and in civil society. Since her way of life was completely uncharacteristic for a woman of her time, Catherine assured those who criticized her that it most definitely was not of her own choosing but, rather, was "from the Holy Spirit." Filling Catherine with the "consuming flame" of "burning charity," the Holy Spirit inspired her to preach and to undertake works of love and service to others, as well as missions of Church reform and civil reconciliation. The Holy Spirit also gave her the strength to make the rigorous journeys needed to accomplish some of these missions. Her great vitality, Raymond of Capua tells us, came

---

[93] St. Cyril of Jerusalem, *Catechetical Lectures* 21.2.
[94] Bl. Raymond of Capua, *Life*, no. 49, pp. 46, 47.

only from the Holy Spirit, who "exults" in works of charity, such as those that He inspired Catherine to undertake.[95]

In Catherine's letters, we glimpse the depths of her intimacy with the Holy Spirit. One of her most tender names for the Holy Spirit is "Compassionate Mercy." Referring often to the "gentle mercy" of the Holy Spirit, Catherine speaks of the "good inspirations and sweet desires" given "by the Holy Spirit's mercy."[96] In one lovely image, she describes the Holy Spirit as the gentle "waiter" serving us the Banquet of the Lord's precious Body and Blood. Catherine pictures the Father as the lavish "Table" on which the Lord Jesus gives "Himself to us as Food with such burning love." And who is the One who "brought Him to us," the One who "serves" us this precious Banquet of Love? Only the Holy Spirit, who, "because of His boundless love" for us, "is not satisfied to have any one else wait on us" and who "wants to serve as waiter himself."[97]

We also learn from Catherine's letters how completely she depended on the Holy Spirit's guidance. On one of her journeys, she promises that she will return "as soon as the Holy Spirit allows"; and in another letter she writes: "We will do whatever the Holy Spirit will have us do."[98] When Catherine is asked to mediate an important reconciliation, she responds that although she is completely inadequate to the task, she will gladly undertake

---

[95] Ibid., nos. 87, 166, 171; pp. 80, 160, 165.

[96] St. Catherine of Siena, Letters T 94, T 241, T 72, in *The Letters of Catherine of Siena*, vol. 2, trans. Suzanne Noffke, O.P. (Tempe, AZ: Arizona Center for Medieval and Renaissance Studies, 2001), pp. 671, 209, 331.

[97] St. Catherine of Siena, Letter T 52, in *Letters*, vol. 2, p. 120.

[98] St. Catherine of Siena, Letters T 124, T 115, in *Letters*, vol. 2, pp. 698, 370.

whatever mission the Holy Spirit permits her to accept. In still another beautiful letter, she writes: "Whatever you have to do or say, rehearse it first between God and you in holy prayer." Our "Teacher" dwelling within us is "the Holy Spirit who is Mercy." "He will pour into you a light of wisdom that will make you discern and choose what will honor God."[99]

Catherine had no formal education, but she longed to learn how to read and write so that she could pray the Divine Office and express in writing the sentiments the Holy Spirit placed within her. The Holy Spirit not only gave her these desires, but also fulfilled them without the intermediary of a human teacher. As Catherine herself confesses, it was by divine help that she learned to read and write, abilities that she used with such wisdom that, although she had no schooling, she has been honored as one of the first two women Doctors of the Church.

Catherine recounted to her dear friend Raymond of Capua how she was given the gift to read. A companion had tried to help her to learn, but these efforts came to nothing. Undaunted, Catherine asked the Lord Himself to teach her to read. If this was not the Lord's will, she would "gladly remain illiterate." Her fervent prayer was answered, and, without any human teacher, she began to read, a gift that filled her heart with joy.[100]

In a precious letter to Raymond, Catherine recounts also how she learned to write. She confesses that she is "in torment" because of so many sins committed against the goodness of God, and because there is no one to whom she can "unburden" her soul about her distress. Catherine adds, however, this wonderful news:

[99] St. Catherine of Siena, Letters T 123, T 267, in Letters, vol. 2, pp. 376, 474.
[100] Bl. Raymond of Capua, Life, no. 113; pp. 104, 105.

"The Holy Spirit has provided for me interiorly by His mercy, and outwardly has provided for me a diversion in writing." She joyously reveals that the wonderful "refreshment" of being able to write, a "consolation" she had never known before because of her "ignorance," was given to her in a "marvelous manner" by the Holy Spirit Himself.[101]

We see in Catherine a wonderful example of how the Holy Spirit lovingly inspires our prayer by teaching and guiding us and also by drawing us to savor the Trinity's loving presence in our souls. Regardless of what we are called to do throughout the day, if we dwell with the Divine Persons, who make Their home within us (John 14:23), we will find, as Catherine did, the peace and joy of the Kingdom of God in our souls (Luke 17:21).

As our own intimacy with the Holy Spirit grows, we find that our love for Our Blessed Mother also deepens, for she is the beloved spouse of the Holy Spirit.[102] In our needs, the Holy Spirit inspires us to turn to Our Blessed Mother as our very own Mother (John 19:27), who longs to enfold us in her powerful help and tender care. Inspired by the Holy Spirit, we treasure the gift of praying the Rosary, a prayer that can fill us with such peace that we may be unable even to finish the words and be drawn simply to rest in the Trinity's presence within us.

To nourish our prayer, the Holy Spirit also gives us a deepened love for Scripture and for the writings of the saints. It is the Holy Spirit who increases our desire to attend Mass more frequently, to receive the precious gift of the Lord Jesus in the Eucharist, and even to pray the Liturgy of the Hours, nourishing our souls

[101] St. Catherine of Siena, Letter T 272, in *Letters*, vol. 2, p. 505.
[102] St. Louis Grignion de Montfort, *True Devotion to the Blessed Virgin*, no. 4.

with Sacred Scripture and with writings of the saints. We may be drawn to pray treasured prayers, litanies, and novenas or to sing aloud or in our hearts beautiful hymns that anoint our souls with the Holy Spirit's peace and joy. St. Paul urges us to be filled with gratitude as we "sing psalms, hymns, and spiritual songs to God" (Col. 3:16). St. Augustine, too, encourages us to pray with a song in our hearts: "Listen to the Holy Spirit saying through me ... sing with your voices, your hearts ... your lives."[103]

As we grow in the habit of praying throughout the day, asking for the Holy Spirit's help and anointing upon our every breath, we begin to see the beautiful fruits of prayer blossom in our lives. With the Holy Spirit's love filling our hearts, peace and joy replace worry and anxiety, and distress gives way to the Holy Spirit's contentment, filling our souls like a "feast" (Ps. 63:5). May we desire these beautiful fruits of prayer, trusting that the habit of praying "without ceasing" (1 Thess. 5:17) is a precious gift from the Holy Spirit, who never ceases to intercede for us "with sighs too deep for words" (Rom. 8:26).

[103] St. Augustine, Sermon 34, Office of Readings, Tuesday of the Third Week of Easter.

4

Our Healer and Comforter

~✻~

The Holy Spirit, Our Healer

One invaluable way of deepening our intimacy with the Holy Spirit is to invite Him into the most vulnerable places within us. Even as we enjoy countless blessings, we cannot help struggling, in ways large and small, with pain and fears, worries and regrets, with wounds of the past and difficulties in the present. In the Sequence for the Mass of Pentecost, we entrust to the Holy Spirit all that causes us pain, imploring Him to renew our strength and to heal our every wound. The parable of the Good Samaritan (Luke 10:29–37) gives us a striking intimation of the Holy Spirit's power as our Healer. A traveler falls among thieves, who rob and beat him, but a Samaritan has pity on him. Binding up the traveler's wounds, the Samaritan entrusts him to an innkeeper to nurse him to full health. In this beautiful parable we see reflected the compassion of the Lord Jesus, who binds up our wounds through His saving death and Resurrection and then entrusts us to His tender Holy Spirit to bring us to full healing.[104]

[104] St. Irenaeus, *Against Heresies* 3.17.3.

Drawing Close to the Holy Spirit

Like the traveler in the Gospel account, we, too, can fall victim to inner thieves that rob us of our peace and joy. Surely, gratitude fills our hearts for all of our blessings, and yet none of us is a stranger to physical, emotional, mental, or spiritual pain. We know what it is to grieve the death of loved ones, to miss family and friends who are far away, to feel lonely and sad, to be wounded by those who have hurt us, and to suffer from illness and physical distress. We naturally recoil from pain and rightly seek ways to alleviate it. As we seek freedom and healing, the Holy Spirit inspires us not only to use the help of wise physicians and counselors but also to hand ourselves over to His tender care. St. Ambrose of Milan reminds us that the infinitely powerful Holy Spirit is the One who "breathes" into us "tranquility of mind" and "peace of soul."[105]

It is a cause of thanksgiving that many of us have already entrusted ourselves to the Holy Spirit's healing care and have received, more than once, beautiful answers to our prayers. We may have experienced physical and emotional healing, felt the joy of seeing hearts and lives changed for the good, and witnessed how truly the Holy Spirit can and does free us from past hurts and present pain. These miracles of love encourage us to *keep* turning to the Holy Spirit to implore His healing power for ourselves and those dear to us. If we have never thought of praying to the Holy Spirit for healing, may we do so at this very moment. Let us entrust ourselves and our loved ones, our hurts and pains and all that is not well in our bodies and souls, to the Holy Spirit of Love, asking for His tender healing in every aspect of our lives.

As we learn from experience, our prayer does not need many words. Let us simply ask the Holy Spirit to heal us and our loved

---

[105] St. Ambrose of Milan, *On the Mysteries* 3.11.

ones, to free our minds and hearts, to heal our bodies and souls, our thoughts and memories, our emotions and desires. The Holy Spirit may inspire us to offer this prayer not only in the secret of our hearts but also in prayer spoken aloud and shared with one another: "Most Holy Spirit, please heal me; heal us and those dear to us. All of our trust is in You. Give us Your own peace, freedom, and joy."

In our prayer for healing, the Holy Spirit may draw us to rest in our Blessed Mother's arms, letting her love us with a perfect mother's love. We also may be drawn to cherish our Father's embrace, delighting in His infinite love for us as His precious children. The Holy Spirit may inspire us to rest in the heart of the Lord Jesus, finding in His sacred wounds the healing for our pain of mind, heart, soul, and body. Regardless of the ways the Holy Spirit draws us to pray for healing, our prayers are never wasted, for the Holy Spirit Himself is interceding for us (Rom. 8:26).[106]

As we pray for healing, the Holy Spirit also inspires us to do as the Church does every Easter, when, as an entire community, we "renounce Satan and all his pomps and works." The Lord Jesus freed and healed others by commanding demons to depart from them (Mark 9:17–29; Matt. 12:22–28; Luke 8:26–39).[107] Like those whom Jesus freed, we, too, can face attacks by evil spirits, who try to steal from us our peace and joy. Relying on the power of Jesus, and with words such as the following, let us command to depart from us and our loved ones all evil spirits attempting to rob us of our joy: "In the name of the Lord Jesus, be gone from me, evil spirits attacking me with ... pain, with

---

[106] St. Augustine, Letter 130, to Proba, 15:28.
[107] See also Mark 5:1–20; 6:13; 7:24–30; Matt 8:28–34; Luke 11:14–23.

fear and anxiety, with depression and sadness, with anger, addiction, and sinful habits.... Most sweet Holy Spirit, *free* me and my loved ones, and fill us with Your strength and healing, Your peace and joy." Such prayer to the Holy Spirit, by whose infinite power evil spirits are brought into subjection, can never be without its healing effect in our lives.

It is true that, for reasons we may not understand until we are in Heaven, some of us are permitted to suffer, even throughout our lives, from illnesses and serious afflictions. As we seek healing remedies for our pain, we still may have to deal with physical, mental, or emotional challenges that make us cry out, "How can a good God permit this suffering?" When St. Thomas Aquinas pondered this profound question, he was inspired to understand that if all evil and suffering were removed from our world, far greater good also would be lost.[108] With our human nature wounded by original sin, selfishness comes easily to us. In difficult times, we can receive priceless blessings that we would gain in no other way. Upheld by the Trinity's grace, we can grow in precious virtues, such as deeper trust, compassion, patience, and self-giving love. We rethink what is valuable to us and begin to focus our time and energy on what is truly precious in our lives: our Faith, our families and loved ones, our vocations, our calling to do good with our lives.

When our valiant efforts to gain healing for ourselves or our loved ones seem to be futile, let us pray for the grace to realize that our suffering *does* have a profound meaning and an irreplaceable purpose for good. The Lord Jesus Himself implored His Father to remove the cup of suffering from Him. Even more, however, He desired that His Father's sweet and perfect will would be

---

[108] St. Thomas Aquinas, *Summa Theologiae* I.22.2, ad 2.

accomplished in Him (Matt. 26:39). And so it was on His own Cross of suffering that Jesus won for us the priceless gift of our salvation.

In the Trinity's sacred plan of love for us, pain that we are permitted to suffer in union with the Lord's redemptive suffering is meant to bear fruit in the priceless blessings of our self-giving love here on earth and our ecstatic joy in Heaven. St. Paul assures us that "the sufferings of this present time are not worth comparing with the glory about to be revealed to us" (Rom. 8:18). One day, we *will* see with gladness the immense good won through pain that we could not alleviate, pain suffered in union with the Lord, pain that "unleashed" in us precious virtues such as self-giving love, patience, and compassion toward others in their own pain.[109] In Heaven's bliss, our tears *will* be turned into joy, as we see how absolutely everything that the Trinity's providence permitted for us and our loved ones did, indeed, "work together for good" (Rom. 8:28). We will thrill with joy to see that all that we were permitted to undergo here on earth brought us exquisite blessings that we never would have gained without passing through the crucible of suffering.

One irreplaceable blessing that the Holy Spirit wants for us is the grace of a free and peaceful heart. "Do not grieve the Holy Spirit of God.... Put away from you all bitterness ... anger ... all malice.... Be kind to one another, tenderhearted, forgiving one another" (Eph. 4:30–32). Forgiveness of ourselves and others is not only a beautiful fruit but also an indispensable condition of experiencing the Holy Spirit's peace and healing in our hearts. Our very power to forgive comes from the Holy Spirit, whose

---

[109] St. John Paul II, Apostolic Letter on the Christian Meaning of Human Suffering *Salvifici Doloris* (February 11, 1984), no. 31.

intimate love for us can and does heal even the most wounded places within us. The Holy Spirit is the One who inspires and enables us to forgive, drawing us to pray for conversion and healing in ourselves and in those who have caused us pain. We know that forgiveness does not mean condoning, enabling, or excusing our own or others' sins, nor does it always mean renewed relationships or reconciliation here on earth. It does mean, as St. Paul tells us, a heart freed from bitterness and malice toward those who have hurt us, and the beautiful fruits of serenity, joy, and peace in our souls (Eph. 4:1–3).

In praying to the Holy Spirit for the grace to forgive, we learn by experience that "where the Spirit of the Lord" is, there, truly, is freedom (2 Cor. 3:17). Through His most tender love for us, the Holy Spirit wants to, can, and does free us from our past and present sins as well as from bitterness toward those who have wounded us, even grievously. The saints encourage us by their example. Before his conversion to the Lord, Saul sought out and persecuted Christians, even approving of the murder of the deacon Stephen. The dying Stephen, however, "filled with the Holy Spirit," forgave Saul (Acts 7:59–60), surely winning in this way the grace of Saul's conversion. Now, in Heaven, St. Paul and St. Stephen are intimate friends, bound together by the Holy Spirit's tender love.

The example of saints such as Stephen inspires us to ask for the Holy Spirit's grace of forgiveness in our own hearts, in those we have hurt, and in those who have hurt us. Such prayer can never be fruitless. In ways we could not have anticipated and perhaps will never see here on earth, our prayer *will* gain the Holy Spirit's healing and freedom for us and for those for whom we pray. In Heaven's joy, the Holy Spirit's love *will* make whole all that has been wounded and estranged here on earth.

The Holy Spirit's Healing Power in the Sacraments

The Holy Spirit inspires us to pray for healing not only through our personal prayer but also and especially through receiving the Church's own beautiful sacraments. The most intimate and powerful sacrament for our healing is the precious Body and Blood of the Lord Jesus in the Eucharist. At every Mass we pray, "Lord, say but the word and my soul shall be *healed*." And in the Divine Liturgies of St. John Chrysostom and of St. Basil the Great, the gathered community prays with one heart and one soul before receiving the precious Body and Blood of the Lord in the Eucharist: "May the partaking of your Holy mysteries, O Lord, be not for my judgment or condemnation, but for the healing of my soul and body."[110] It is through the sacred mystery of the Mass and the precious sacrament of the Eucharist that the healing power of the Lord Jesus fills us most wondrously, for the Eucharist *is* Jesus Himself, the infinite Font of love and healing.

It is a joy to realize that the Holy Spirit also is intimately at work to heal us whenever we are present at Mass. The Eucharistic prayer that the celebrant solemnly prays illumines how central the Holy Spirit is in the Eucharistic celebration. In the Second Eucharistic Prayer, the celebrant prays for the descent of the Holy Spirit upon the Eucharistic elements in an especially beautiful way: "Make holy, therefore, these gifts we pray by sending down your Spirit upon them like the dewfall." The Third Eucharistic Prayer, too, implores the Father, "By the same Spirit graciously make holy these gifts we have brought to

---

[110] "Prayer before Communion," St. Michael's Byzantine Catholic Church, https://stmichaelsbyzantine.com/our-faith/prayer-before-communion/.

you for consecration." And, in the Fourth Eucharistic Prayer the celebrant prays, "May this same Holy Spirit graciously sanctify these offerings, that they may become the Body and Blood of our Lord Jesus Christ."[111]

This invoking of the Holy Spirit upon the Eucharistic gifts is particularly striking in the Divine Liturgy of St. John Chrysostom, in which the celebrant implores the Father, "Send down your Holy Spirit upon *us* and upon these gifts lying before us." In this invocation of the Holy Spirit, or *Epiclesis*, the celebrant prays, "Make this bread the precious body of your Christ, and that which is in this chalice the precious blood of your Christ, changing them by your Holy Spirit." It is striking that in the Byzantine Rite Divine Liturgy, the Holy Spirit is invoked not only on the Eucharistic gifts but also upon *us*. The celebrant prays to the Father that those who receive the precious Body and Blood of the Lord may receive "the remission of sins, the communion of your Holy Spirit, the fullness of the heavenly kingdom, and confidence in you."[112] May this beautiful prayer inspire us to pray for the Lord's healing and for the Holy Spirit's loving "communion" every time we receive the most precious Body and Blood of the Lord in the Eucharist.

The sacrament of Penance and Reconciliation is another powerful means of healing for us, not only for our sins but also for the pain and wounds that often cause our sins. It was by pouring out the Holy Spirit upon His apostles that the Lord Jesus instituted

[111] Eucharistic Prayers I–IV, *Roman Missal*, 3rd ed. (2011), Catholic Resources for Bible, Liturgy, Art, and Theology, http://catholic-resources.org/ChurchDocs/RM3-EP1-4.htm.

[112] Anaphora of St. John Chrysostom, Byzantine Catholic Archeparchy of Pittsburgh, https://mci.archpitt.org/liturgy/Divine_Liturgy_Anaphora_Chrysostom.html.

this wonderful sacrament of mercy: "Receive the Holy Spirit. If you forgive the sins of any, they are forgiven" (John 20:22–23). This is why saints such as Basil the Great assure us that our sins are forgiven through the *Holy Spirit*,[113] and the Church's own Liturgy proclaims that "the Spirit himself is the remission of all sins."[114] In the sacrament of Penance and Reconciliation, the Holy Spirit continues to free us from our sins and to heal the wounds and pain that can lead us into sin.

Every time we receive the sacrament of Reconciliation, the Lord Jesus, through the ministry of the priest or bishop, gives us a glorious new outpouring of His Holy Spirit of Love to impart to us His own forgiveness and healing. Even our very *desire* to receive this sacrament of forgiveness comes only from our being tenderly "moved by the Holy Spirit." It is also the Holy Spirit who enables us to realize what is sinful in our lives. We know how easy it is for us to make excuses for our sins, to deny or ignore the fact that what we are choosing to think, desire, or do is sinful. The Holy Spirit's tender mercy, however, "convicts" us of sin, giving us the grace to recognize our sins (John 16:8) and truly to repent of them. The Holy Spirit enables us to confess our sins with heartfelt sorrow and humbly to resolve, with the Holy Spirit's grace, not to sin again. For these very reasons, the Rite of Penance encourages both priests and penitents, as they prepare for the celebration of the sacrament of Reconciliation, to pray for the Holy Spirit's wisdom and love.[115]

In the formula of absolution used in the Roman Rite, the celebrant proclaims that the "Father of mercies" (2 Cor. 1:3), who

---

[113] St. Basil the Great, *On the Holy Spirit* 19.49.
[114] "Prayer over the Gifts," Mass for the Seventh Saturday of Easter.
[115] *Rite of Penance*, nos. 6, 15.

has reconciled us to Himself through His beloved Son's death and Resurrection, has "sent the *Holy Spirit* among us for the forgiveness of sins." In this wonderful sacrament of healing, bishops and priests, "in the name of Christ and by the power of the *Holy Spirit,*" "declare and grant the forgiveness of sins:" "May God give you pardon and peace, and I absolve you from your sins in the name of the Father, and of the Son, and of the Holy Spirit."[116]

Wondrous sacrament of mercy! Through the sacred words of the confessor, Jesus Himself forgives us, and we are made *free* by the power of the Holy Spirit! Because of the healing grace of this precious sacrament, absolutely nothing sinful in our lives has the power to destroy us. St. Catherine of Siena assures us that, in this sacrament of mercy, the Lord Jesus Himself, through the confessor, mystically "pours" over us His most precious Blood in such profusion that it becomes a sacred "bath" for us, washing us *clean* of all of our sins: "Though your sins are like scarlet, they shall be like snow" (Isa. 1:18). Bathed in the Blood of Jesus, we are immersed in the Father's infinite mercy, which is "incomparably greater than all the sins that anyone could commit," and we are filled with the blazing "fire" of the Holy Spirit's "burning charity."[117]

In this beautiful sacrament, the Lord Jesus Himself takes us into His arms, the Father tenderly embraces us, and the Holy Spirit sanctifies us completely. Set free from sins that have enslaved us in the past and those that hold sway over us in the

---

[116] Ibid., nos. 7, 9; *Catechism of the Catholic Church* (CCC), no. 1449.
[117] St. Catherine of Siena, *The Dialogue*, trans. Suzanne Noffke, O.P. (New York: Paulist Press, 1980), nos. 75, 134, 131, 132, 84; pp. 138, 276, 264, 268, 155.

present, we also receive the Holy Spirit's power to avoid future sins. We are not only freed but also made truly *holy*. Giving Himself to us to dwell "more fully" within us, the Holy Spirit thus transforms us ever more deeply into His living, holy "temple" (1 Cor. 6:19). As the culmination of the healing grace of this sacrament, the Holy Spirit draws us to the sacred mystery of the Mass. There, the forgiveness we have received in the sacrament of Reconciliation is wonderfully "expressed" by our fervently receiving the Lord Jesus in the Eucharist, in this way bringing "great joy" to "the banquet of God's Church."[118]

Let us pray for the grace to make frequent use of this beautiful sacrament of mercy, in which the Holy Spirit's forgiveness and healing are poured out so wonderfully into our souls. May we continue to pray for freedom and healing from sinful habits over which we may have been powerless in the past, but which can be and *are* conquered by the infinite power of the Holy Spirit, who ceaselessly "fights for us"![119]

Another precious instrument of the Holy Spirit's healing is the sacrament of the Anointing of the Sick. In this tender sacrament, the Holy Spirit comes to bring us healing, often for our physical suffering and always for our emotional and spiritual pain. This truly is a "sacrament for the sick" and not only for those near death. In the blessing of oil used for the Anointing of the Sick, the bishop prays that the Holy Spirit, our Comforter, Helper, and intimate "Friend," will consecrate the oil, so that those anointed with it may grow strong and well in every part of their being. In administering this beautiful sacrament, the celebrant anoints us and prays that our entire person may be healed, strengthened,

---

[118] *Rite of Penance*, no. 6
[119] St. Cyril of Jerusalem, *Catechetical Lectures* 16.16, 19, 20.

comforted, and freed from all anxiety, especially about death, "through the grace of the Holy Spirit."[120]

Countless people have experienced the great joy of physical healing through the power of this sacrament. We know that it also may be the Trinity's plan of love to bring healing that is spiritual and emotional but not necessarily physical. Many of us have seen fear and anxiety give way to a beautiful serenity in dying loved ones who have received this precious sacrament, with family members and others present uniting themselves to the celebrant's prayer. The calming grace of this beautiful sacrament is all the more evident if we also command any evil spirits attacking our dying loved ones with fear and anxiety to depart from them in the name of the Lord Jesus. When we or those dear to us are sick, or preparing for the sacred encounter with the Lord that is death, let us turn to this precious sacrament to receive the Holy Spirit's healing, peace, comfort, and strength.

Our Consoler and Comforter

In all of our trials, the Holy Spirit is not only our intimate Healer but also our tender Consoler and Comforter. The Lord Himself promised to send us the Holy Spirit as the "Paraclete," our "Counselor" and "Advocate" (John 14:16–17, 26; 16:7), who defends us and fights for us. Because the Holy Spirit is also our Helper who fiercely protects us, Church Fathers such as St. Cyril of Jerusalem called the Paraclete our strong and mighty "Comforter."[121]

[120] *Pastoral Care of the Sick: Rites of Anointing and Viaticum*, nos. 6, 25.
[121] St. Cyril of Jerusalem, *Catechetical Lectures* 16.3.

Reflecting on how truly the Holy Spirit, our Beloved Friend, is also our Comforter in every difficulty, St. Thomas Aquinas recalls to us how protected and consoled we are by our friends who truly love us. What joy it gives us to be with them! We delight in their dear presence, enjoying what they say and do and finding strength in their love for us. In all of our troubles, "we hasten to our friends for consolation." In this, our own experience of close friendship, Thomas finds a beautiful reflection of the Holy Spirit, our Beloved Friend, the *Best* of Consolers, through whom "we have joy in God and security against all the world's adversities and assaults."[122]

The early Christians lived always in the consoling presence and "comfort of the Holy Spirit" (Acts 9:31), our Paraclete and dear "Consoler" who "takes away our pain and sadness and gives us joy in divine things." In our every hardship, the Holy Spirit wants to strengthen *us* with His grace, fill *us* with His peace, and comfort *us* with His tender love. If we hand over everything in our lives to the Holy Spirit, we, too, like the early Christians, will know the happiness of living always in the sweet "consolation of the Holy Spirit."[123]

In a special way, the Holy Spirit is our intimate Consoler in the face of death. When we grieve the death of loved ones, the Holy Spirit tenderly comforts us with His love,[124] assuring us of the "glorious inheritance among the saints" to which we and our

---

[122] St. Thomas Aquinas, *Summa Contra Gentiles* IV.22.3. In *Summa Contra Gentiles*, bk. 4, *Salvation*, trans. Charles J. O'Neil, (New York: Hanover House, 1957), https://isidore.co/aquinas/ContraGentiles4.htm#22.

[123] St. Thomas Aquinas, *Commentary on John* 15, lecture 5, no. 2060; *Summa Contra Gentiles*, IV.22.3.

[124] St. Cyril of Jerusalem, *Catechetical Lectures* 16.3, 20.

loved ones have been called (Eph. 1:13, 18). Even in our grief, the Holy Spirit enables us to experience the precious reality of the Communion of Saints, whose very heart is the Holy Spirit of Love.[125] It is the Holy Spirit who deepens our faith that our dear ones who have died are far closer to us now, praying for and helping us, caring for and protecting us. The Holy Spirit consoles us, too, with the assurance that we *shall* see again our loved ones who have died into the Trinity's mercy. We will hold them again and delight in their sweet embrace forever!

The same Holy Spirit who dwells so lovingly within us now as our Comforter also will be our Consolation and Strength at our own death. It is at this sacred moment that we most need the Holy Spirit's grace to surrender ourselves into the embrace of our heavenly Father. We are greatly consoled by St. John of the Cross, who writes that those who intimately love the Holy Spirit now can hope and trust that their death will be "very gentle and very sweet."[126] Let us then pray to the Holy Spirit, who is the "Strength of the weak," the "Help of the afflicted," and the "Hope of the dying,"[127] that we and our loved ones will be blessed with a death full of the Holy Spirit's most sweet love and tender peace. Let us pray also for the grace to trust that not only in every joy but also in every distress that we have experienced or may encounter in the future, the Holy Spirit will turn everything to the good (Rom. 8:28). Enfolding us in His love, the Holy Spirit, our Comforter, is at work in every event of our lives, gently drawing us home to Heaven's joy.

[125] CCC 948.

[126] St. John of the Cross, *The Living Flame of Love* 1.35, 36, 30; pp. 594, 595, 592.

[127] Prayer for the Indwelling of the Spirit, attributed to St. Augustine.

Pledge of Heaven's Joy

We have been created for the wonders of Heaven, but even now we have within us the infinitely sweet Gift of the Holy Spirit, who is, in Person, the living "pledge" and "guarantee" of Heaven's joy (2 Cor. 1:22, 5:4–5; Eph. 1:14). A pledge or guarantee of a future good is its beginning in us now, received as the assurance of our one day possessing it entirely. We may think of a marvelous treasure that its owner promises to give us. As a pledge that we can trust this promise, the owner gives us the central portion of the treasure, as well as the key that alone will open the treasure. In some way, then, the whole treasure is already ours through the pledge we have received. The Holy Spirit poured out by the risen Lord Jesus is the beautiful, living "Pledge" of Heaven and the beginning of Heaven even now in our hearts.

Amazing mystery of love! In the Holy Spirit, the future blessings promised to us are, in a profound way, already ours! St. Paul describes as the "fruit" of the Holy Spirit marvelous gifts so sweet to our souls that they allow us to savor in some way the Holy Spirit's own goodness: "love, joy, peace, patience, kindness, generosity, faithfulness, gentleness, and self-control" (Gal. 5:22–23). Infinitely more wondrous even than the Holy Spirit's "fruit," however, is the intimate presence of the Holy Spirit Himself, who is, in Person, the living "foretaste and promise of the paschal feast of heaven."[128] St. Basil the Great tells us that it is through the Holy Spirit's tender and faithful love that our "hearts are lifted up, the weak are held by the hand," and those who are "advancing are brought to perfection." The Holy Spirit, who is our beloved Friend and the Giver of all good gifts, is also the One who imparts to us "heavenly citizenship, a place in the

---

[128] "Preface VI of Sundays in Ordinary Time."

chorus of angels, joy without end," and the incredible grace of "abiding in God."[129]

In a word, St. Basil assures us, through the Holy Spirit, "*every blessing* is showered upon us," not only in this world, but also "in the world to come." The Spirit of Life, who "gives life" to us now through grace, is also the One who imparts risen life to us at the end of time (Rom. 8:2; John 6:63): "He who raised Christ from the dead will give life to your mortal bodies also through his Spirit" dwelling "in you" (Rom. 8:11). Let us then ask the Holy Spirit to preserve us in His tender grace here on earth, so that, at our death, He truly may lead us home to Heaven's joy.[130]

We voice our desire for this ecstatic bliss of Heaven when, in the Our Father, we pray, "Your kingdom come" (Luke 11:2). In some early manuscripts, this petition is replaced with the intimate prayer, "May your *Spirit* come upon us and purify us." St. Gregory of Nyssa beautifully comments about this alternate wording: "Sweet is the voice by which we bring this petition before God," for the Holy Spirit, who "cleanses us and forgives our sins," *is*, in a profound way, the "Kingdom" promised to us in the Lord's Prayer.[131] May we who have been sealed with the Holy Spirit unto the day of redemption (Eph. 4:30) find our strength and contentment even now in the heavenly "Kingdom" within us, the Holy Spirit, who is our Healing, Comfort, and Joy.

---

[129] St. Basil the Great, *On the Holy Spirit* 9.23, 15.36.

[130] Ibid, 16.40.

[131] St. Gregory of Nyssa, Homily 3 on the Lord's Prayer: *Hallowed Be Thy Name, Thy Kingdom Come*, trans. Theodore G. Stylianopoulos (2003),Orthodox Prayer, https://www.orthodoxprayer.org/Articles_files/Lord's%20Prayer/3.%20Hallowed%20Be.pdf.

5

Intimacy with the Holy Spirit and Our Baptism and Confirmation

ﻣ

In this final chapter, we reflect on two wondrous sacraments whose graces are an indispensable means of deepening our intimacy with the Holy Spirit. Every Sunday we make this beautiful profession of faith: "I believe in the Holy Spirit, the Lord, the Giver of Life" (cf. John 6:63)![132] In these wonderful words, we proclaim our belief in the Holy Spirit's presence and power lavished on us in our Baptism and Confirmation.

The magnificent sacrament of Baptism unites us to the Lord's death and Resurrection, filling us with sanctifying grace through which the Divine Persons make Their intimate home within us (John 14:23). Confirmation, beautifully named the "Mystery of Chrismation" by Eastern Rite Christians, "completes" our Baptism and unites us to the glorious event of Pentecost, the "completion" of the Lord's death, Resurrection, and Ascension. It is through Confirmation that we are irrevocably "sealed" with the Holy Spirit so that we forever "belong" to Him. We also receive in this sacrament the grace truly to enjoy, as the apostles

---

[132] Nicene-Constantinopolitan Creed.

did after Pentecost, the Holy Spirit's sweet "familiarity" and intimate friendship.[133] Beautiful mystery of love! Intimacy with the Holy Spirit is so crucial to our life in Christ that we receive for this very purpose a sacrament central to our Christian initiation!

The Treasures of Our Baptism

In order to appreciate more fully the wonders of our being intimately sealed with the Holy Spirit in Confirmation, we consider first the sacrament of Baptism, which Confirmation exquisitely "completes." Baptism, the foundation for receiving every other sacrament, unites us to the Lord's death, which has conquered our sin and death. Inseparably, it also immerses us in His glorious Resurrection as the source of our life of grace. Through this precious gift of sanctifying grace, the divine Persons of the Trinity dwell intimately in our souls, and we are changed from creatures into beloved sons and daughters of the Father, brothers and sisters of the Lord, and sacred temples of the Holy Spirit. These tremendous blessings fill us through the marvelous activity of the Holy Spirit (Rom. 8:9, 15), who transforms us at our Baptism into "Christians" (Acts 11:26), those who are "anointed" with the Holy Spirit.[134]

It was in this intimate "anointing" of the Holy Spirit that the Lord Jesus lived His life, suffered His Passion and death, and rose in glory at His Resurrection, all for our sake, so that "from His fullness" *we* might all receive (John 1:16). Conceived by the

---

[133] St. Thomas Aquinas, *Commentary on the Gospel of John* 14, lecture 4, n. 1920; "Prayer for Terce," Tuesday of Week I in Ordinary Time.

[134] St. Thomas Aquinas, *Commentary on the Gospel of John* 3, lecture 1, no. 442.

power of the Holy Spirit and "anointed" with the Holy Spirit after His symbolic baptism by John (Luke 1:35; 3:21–22), the Lord "rejoiced in the Holy Spirit" (Luke 10:21), preached and cast out demons (Matt. 12:28), offered His suffering and death to the Father, and rose gloriously from the dead, all in the tender power of the same Holy Spirit (Heb. 9:14; Rom. 8:11).

This is not because the Lord Jesus needed the Holy Spirit, for He is God the Son. It was for *our* sake that the Father anointed His Son's human nature with the Holy Spirit, so that *we* could receive the Holy Spirit from the Lord. How fitting that the Holy Spirit promised to us in our sacramental Baptism (Mark 1:8; Matt. 3:11) first would anoint the humanity of the Savior, who then would bestow the Holy Spirit upon us![135] The Lord Jesus Himself assures us that we can enter the Kingdom of Heaven only when we are "born again of water and *Spirit*" (John 3:5). It was not to sanctify the Lord, therefore, that the Holy Spirit descended upon Him after His Baptism. Rather, it was to prefigure *our* Baptism and to make holy the baptismal waters in which *we* would be reborn in the Holy Spirit.

How tremendous are the supernatural life and power that fill us when we are born again of water and of the Holy Spirit in Baptism! As the water encompasses our bodies, our souls are flooded with the Holy Spirit, the Living Water of Life. The Holy Spirit in this way baptizes not only our bodies but also our souls, "within, and completely," entering into "the inmost recesses" of our souls and flowing from us as "rivers of living water" (John 7:38). The baptismal font thus serves as a grave for our human nature, wounded by sin, and as a second womb, bringing us to supernatural birth as beloved sons and daughters of our Father

---

[135] St. Cyril of Jerusalem, *Catechetical Lectures* 17.9.

in the Lord Jesus.[136] Even those who have been enslaved by the most wretched of sins emerge from the baptismal waters completely cleansed, filled with the Holy Spirit's power to be free![137]

Innocent babies and children also are meant to receive these wonders of baptismal grace, for they, too, are created not only for natural blessings but also, and most of all, for the precious gift of the Trinity's divine life. As St. John Chrysostom assures us, "We baptize even infants, although they are sinless," precisely so that, receiving the "gifts of sanctification, justice, filial adoption, and inheritance," they, too, may be "members of Christ, and become dwelling places for the Spirit."[138]

As we have seen, through Baptism, the Holy Spirit fills us with sanctifying grace, a created sharing in the Trinity's divine life. It is through this precious gift of sanctifying grace that the Divine Persons of the Trinity dwell intimately within us and make our souls Their beloved "Home" (John 14:23). Baptism also imparts to us the magnificent theological virtues of faith, hope, and charity as well as the supernatural moral virtues and the wonderful seven gifts of the Holy Spirit. These remarkable blessings bestowed on us by the Holy Spirit, "the Giver of Life" (John 6:63), "surpass all human understanding."[139] And they are available to us at every moment of our lives! Regardless of how young we were when we were baptized, or how old we are when we begin to treasure and cooperate with our baptismal graces, it is never too late to ask the Holy Spirit to bring them to marvelous fruition in us.

[136] Ibid., 17.14, 20.4.
[137] St. John Chrysostom, *Baptismal Instructions*, trans. Paul W. Harkins (New York: Newman Press, 1963), 4.3; pp. 66–67.
[138] Ibid., 3.6; p. 57.
[139] Ibid., 5.22, p. 89.

The Holy Spirit and Our Baptism and Confirmation

The Glorious Celebration of Baptism and Chrismation in the Early Church

We can grasp more deeply the wonders of our Baptism if we reflect on its early Christian celebration, now reclaimed in the beautiful Rite of Christian Initiation of Adults. In the early Church, Baptism often was conferred during the sacred night of the Lord's Resurrection, the Easter Vigil, with rites permeating the community especially with the Holy Spirit's transforming glory. St. John Chrysostom promised his catechumens that this wondrous sacrament would bring them immense "joy and gladness of the Spirit." As they were being immersed in the sacred waters, the Holy Spirit Himself would descend upon them, burying their "old," merely natural self and raising them up full of grace and entirely "new"![140]

Catechumens such as those being taught by St. John Chrysostom underwent a period of careful instruction and fasting in preparation for their Baptism. On the long-awaited all-night Paschal Vigil, they were prayed over with exorcisms, and, supported by the entire community, they renounced Satan and pledged their adherence to Jesus, their Lord. The bishop had invoked the Holy Spirit's outpouring upon the baptismal font to make it a "living spring" filled with the Holy Spirit, who alone "gives life" (2 Cor. 3:6; John 6:63).[141] Into these sacred waters the catechumens then were plunged three times as they were solemnly baptized "in the name of the Father, and of the Son, and of the Holy Spirit." As the Holy Spirit invisibly descended upon them, they died to their old life of sin and rose to wondrous "divine" life in the risen Lord Jesus!

[140] Ibid., 1:1; 2.25, pp. 23, 52.
[141] St. Gregory of Nyssa, *On the Holy Spirit*.

Drawing Close to the Holy Spirit

Clothed in new garments, the newly baptized then were joyfully presented to the bishop, who "completed" their sacramental initiation. Laying hands on them, he fervently prayed over them for the fullness of the "Gift" of the Holy Spirit (Acts 2:38), as he solemnly anointed them with chrism, consecrated oil perfumed with fragrant spices. Having been plunged into the Lord's death and Resurrection, the newly baptized thus were joined to the Lord's own "anointing" by His Father (Acts 10:38) after His symbolic baptism by John (Mark 1:9–11). Inseparably, they also were immersed in the Holy Spirit's glorious outpouring upon the apostles at Pentecost (Acts 2:1–4). After this sacramental anointing and solemn "sealing" with the Holy Spirit (Eph. 1:13), the newly baptized and "chrismated" Christians were presented to the entire community gathered for the Easter Eucharist.

St. John Chrysostom describes the immense joy of the gathered community at the appearance of the newborn Christians: "All who are present embrace them, greet them, kiss them, rejoice with them, and congratulate them." Those who had entered the baptismal waters "slaves and captives" of sin had emerged as beloved sons and daughters, destined to take their place at the royal banquet of their heavenly Father![142]

The procession of the new Christians into the midst of the community evoked a "huge surge of sentiment among the whole gathering as the neophytes — still damp, oily, fragrant, and dressed in new garments" — were led into the assembly. Haunting melodies and jubilant ovations greeted them as they received the community's embrace of welcome into the Trinity's family. Then, with the entire community, the new Christians participated in the Eucharistic celebration of the Lord's Last Supper, through

---

[142] St. John Chrysostom, *Baptismal Instructions* 2.27; p. 53.

which He makes present His own death and Resurrection. As the culmination of their initiation into the Christian life, they feasted on the Lord's precious Body and Blood in the Eucharist. In preparation for sharing in this most sacred Banquet, early Christian communities thus celebrated the richness of Baptism and Chrismation with "enough water to die in," and "oil so fragrant" that it filled the gathered community with the perfume of the Holy Spirit's glorious new life.[143]

The Mystery of Our Confirmation: Sharing in the Grace of Pentecost

"You ... were marked with the seal of the promised Holy Spirit" (Eph. 1:13). We have seen that, in the early Church, the sacrament of Baptism was "completed" by a beautiful sacramental rite of anointing, through which the newly baptized shared in the wondrous outpouring of the Holy Spirit upon the apostles at Pentecost (Acts 2:1–4).[144] It was on that magnificent day that the Holy Spirit, the "Comforter" and "Pilot of the tempest-tossed," had wondrously descended from Heaven as "the Guardian and Sanctifier of the Church."[145]

The Acts of the Apostles overflows with the glorious joy of all that the Holy Spirit accomplished in and through the apostles after Pentecost, when they had been "*filled* with the Holy Spirit" (Acts 2:4). Through the apostles' preaching, growing numbers of people repented, were baptized, and received

---

[143] Aidan Kavanagh, *The Shape of Baptism: The Rite of Christian Initiation* (New York: Pueblo, 1978), pp. 65, 178, 179, 180.

[144] St. Thomas Aquinas, *Summa Theologiae* III.72.7.

[145] St. Cyril of Jerusalem, *Catechetical Lectures* 17.12, 13.

the same tremendous Gift of the Holy Spirit. Becoming "one heart and soul" (Acts 4:32) in the Holy Spirit, the community was built up, as the same Holy Spirit worked miracles of love and healing among them.[146] With the Holy Spirit's power and guidance, the Church spread out from Jerusalem, and growing numbers of Gentiles also experienced the glorious outpouring of the Holy Spirit upon them. Soon, the disciples of the risen Lord came to be known as "Christians" (Acts 11:26), those *"anointed"* with the *Holy Spirit*. The Church continued to grow throughout the empire, with Christians increasingly identified as those "filled with joy and with the Holy Spirit" (Acts 13:52).[147]

Several centuries later, as St. Cyril of Jerusalem was preparing his catechumens to be received into the Church, he promised them that the Holy Spirit's tremendous "Seal of fellowship" soon would be theirs. The same Holy Spirit poured out on the apostles would be lavished on *them*. At Pentecost, the Holy Spirit had *filled* the apostles, who "partook" "of saving fire"; this is the same wondrous outpouring that they should expect![148]

St. Cyril later explained to his newly initiated Christians that everything in their sacramental reception had taken place in union with the Lord, who had been "anointed" with the Holy Spirit after His own symbolic Baptism (Acts 10:38). So, too, the new Christians had been anointed with the Holy Spirit, the living "Oil of Gladness" and Source of all "spiritual gladness." Furthermore, the Holy Spirit had "sealed" (Eph. 1:13) their souls with nothing less than *Himself*, the heavenly "Seal at which evil spirits tremble"![149]

---

[146] Acts 2:38, 43; 4:31–34; 5:12–16.
[147] Acts 8:17; 9:17; 10:17, 38, 44–48; 13:1–4, 46–48.
[148] St. Cyril of Jerusalem, *Catechetical Lectures* 18.33; 17.15.
[149] Ibid., 21.1–3; 4.16; Prologue 17; 17.35.

The Holy Spirit and Our Baptism and Confirmation

Anointed and Sealed with the Holy Spirit

"You ... were marked with the seal of the promised Holy Spirit" (Eph. 1:13). This sacramental "anointing" with the "Seal" of the Holy Spirit after Baptism came to be called the "Mystery of Chrismation" by Eastern Christians and the sacrament of Confirmation by Western Christians. In the West, Confirmation eventually was separated from Baptism so that the bishop could be the usual minister of the sacrament. In the Eastern rites, however, Chrismation and the Eucharist have never been separated from Baptism, including the Baptism of infants, and priests conferring the Mystery of Chrismation do so with chrism consecrated by the bishop. In both East and West, the celebrant prays for a Pentecostal outpouring of the Holy Spirit upon the candidates and anoints them with chrism, olive oil mixed with perfumed spices.

Because it is "soothing to wounds" and makes us "radiant with beauty, health, and strength," olive oil is a wonderful means of symbolizing and of conveying the Holy Spirit's precious anointing.[150] As our bodies are anointed with consecrated, perfumed olive oil at our Confirmation, our souls also are "anointed" with the *living* "Oil of Gladness," the very person of the Holy Spirit, who invisibly "*seals*" our souls with Himself: "In him ... you were marked with the seal of the promised Holy Spirit" (Eph. 1:13). By means of this wondrous sacrament of Confirmation, the Holy Spirit claims us as His very own, so that we belong irrevocably to Him.[151] The *Holy Spirit* thus is the indelible Seal on our souls!

Preparation for Confirmation is immeasurably enriched, therefore, by a focus not only on the deepening of the Holy Spirit's

---

[150] St. Thomas Aquinas, *Summa Theologiae* III.72.2, ad 3
[151] St. Cyril of Jerusalem, *Catechetical Lectures* 3.1–3; 17.35, 36.

gifts and power in us, but also, and most of all, on our receiving in this glorious sacrament the "*fullness*" of the Holy Spirit. In this "mystery of Chrismation," the Holy Spirit gives Himself even more deeply to us, to be completely and fully *possessed* and *enjoyed* by us. As St. Thomas Aquinas beautifully comments, when the Holy Spirit is "sent" to us, as He is in the Pentecostal outpouring we receive at our Confirmation, the Holy Spirit draws us to *Himself*.[152]

Exquisite mystery of love! At our Confirmation, we are blessed to receive the full and lavish outpouring of the Holy Spirit, the Living Gift bestowed on the apostles at Pentecost, the Holy Spirit who "seals" *us* with nothing less than Himself![153] Furthermore, in this sacrament, we receive, as the apostles did at Pentecost, the priceless gift of the Holy Spirit's intimate "familiarity" and friendship as the very source of our power to proclaim the risen Lord with our lives.[154]

"Be Sealed with the Gift of the Holy Spirit"

"Be sealed with the Gift of the Holy Spirit." These are the sacred words now used by Roman-Rite bishops and priests as they anoint candidates with sacred chrism in the conferring of the sacrament of Confirmation. To appreciate more fully the wondrous

---

[152] St. Thomas Aquinas, *Sermon for the Feast of Pentecost,*" no. 2, trans. Peter Kwasniewski and Jeremy Holmes, https://isidore.co/aquinas/Serm11Emitte.htm#text.

[153] St. Thomas Aquinas, *Summa Theologiae* III.72.1, ad 1; III.72.2; I.38.1; CCC 1302.

[154] St. Thomas Aquinas, *Commentary on the Gospel of John* 14, lecture 4, no. 1920; Prayer for Terce, Tuesday of Week I in Ordinary Time.

mystery conveyed through these magnificent words, we consider why Pope St. Paul VI adapted for Confirmation in the Roman Rite the ancient Chrismation formula of the Byzantine Rite, "The Seal of the Gift of the Holy Spirit."

For centuries, the Roman-Rite formula for Confirmation had stressed the reception of the "chrism of salvation" without any reference to being "sealed" by the Holy Spirit Himself. In December 1961, however, the Holy Spirit began a wonderful series of events that would result in the changing of the formula for Confirmation. The Holy Spirit inspired Pope St. John XXIII to pray for a glorious "new Pentecost" upon the Church as he convoked Vatican Council II.[155] After the death of Pope John XXIII two years later, St. Paul VI was elected pope and soon afterward promulgated the Vatican II Constitution on the Sacred Liturgy, whose conciliar decrees included the restoration of the magnificent initiation rites of the early Church.[156]

Eight years later, Pope St. Paul VI himself chose for use in the conferring of Confirmation in the Roman Rite the ancient Chrismation formula of the Byzantine Rite, rendering it almost word for word: "Be sealed with the Gift of the Holy Spirit." The pope explained that he chose this beautiful Byzantine Rite formula not only because it recalls the "Pentecostal outpouring of the Holy Spirit," but also, and most of all, because it expresses "the Gift of the Holy Spirit *himself*." The sacred words, "Be sealed with the Gift of the Holy Spirit," Pope St. Paul VI stressed, make

---

[155] Pope St. John XXIII, Apostolic Constitution Convoking Vatican Council II *Humanae Salutis* (Of Human Salvation) (December 25, 1961).

[156] Second Vatican Council, Constitution on the Sacred Liturgy *Sacrosanctum Concilium* (December 4, 1963), 1.21; 3.64, 66, 71.

clear "the very *essence*" of Confirmation, "through which the faithful receive the *Holy Spirit* as a Gift."[157]

"Be sealed with the Gift of the Holy Spirit!" What a magnificent mystery of love is conveyed in the two parts of this profound sacramental formula! Let us consider the first part: "Be sealed." What do these beautiful words mean? St. John Chrysostom pierces to the heart of the matter when he explains that without the Holy Spirit's sacramental anointing, catechumens are like "sheep without a seal."[158] What a striking image! Sheep "without a seal" have no home, no one to protect them; they are alone and powerless. They belong to no one. In stark contrast, "*sealed*" sheep bear the irrevocable mark or seal of the one to whom they *belong*. Sealed sheep are safe; they have a home and a fierce protector. This beautiful image helps us to understand how, through our Confirmation, we are irrevocably marked by the Holy Spirit's own "seal," the symbol of His complete and total "ownership" of us.[159] Through the sacramental "seal" of Confirmation, we forever "belong" to the Holy Spirit as His very own!

The second part of the Confirmation formula is just as striking: "With the *Gift of the Holy Spirit*." As we have seen, one of the Holy Spirit's most beautiful names is "Gift" (Acts 2:38).[160] We know that a true gift is bestowed on us only through love, and only so that we may truly *possess* and *enjoy* the gift as our very *own*. The renewed formula of Confirmation makes clear that, in Confirmation, we receive a magnificent deepening not only of the Holy Spirit's seven gifts but also, and most importantly, of

---

[157] Pope St. Paul VI, Apostolic Constitution on the Sacrament of Confirmation *Divinae Consortium Naturae* (August 15, 1971).

[158] St. John Chrysostom, *Baptismal Instructions* 10.16; p. 155.

[159] CCC 1295.

[160] St. Thomas Aquinas, *Summa Theologiae* 1.38.2.

the Gift who is the *Holy Spirit Himself*, to *possess* fully and *enjoy* intimately!

Confirmation in this way effects a wonderful *mutual* possession in us: we irrevocably "belong" to the Holy Spirit, and the Holy Spirit irrevocably "belongs" to *us*. As the formula for Confirmation proclaims, we are *sealed* and thus *possessed* by the Holy Spirit, belonging completely to Him. The Holy Spirit, however, also gives *Himself* as Gift to *us*, to *be possessed* by *us* and to belong completely to *us*. Through sanctifying grace, the Holy Spirit dwells within us "as the beloved is in the lover."[161] The Holy Spirit thus *gives Himself* fully to us in Confirmation so that we may completely possess and *enjoy* Him as *our* Gift and *our Beloved*. And what magnificent joy this brings to our souls, for the Holy Spirit *is* the Father and Son's living Sweetness, Their tender Love and intimate Embrace.[162] Astounding mystery of love! We bear within *us* the Father and Son's own intimate "Beloved" as *our* Beloved.

We receive the glorious sacrament of Confirmation only once because, like Baptism, it imprints on our souls an indelible character that cannot be repeated. This sacramental character is a permanent spiritual power that is the very seal of the Holy Spirit irrevocably *consecrating* us for divine worship.[163] Through the wondrous sacrament of Confirmation, we are "consecrated" to the Holy Spirit, to whom we belong and who belongs forever to us. In the beautiful hymn "Come, Creator Spirit," often sung at the conferring of the sacrament of Confirmation, we implore the Holy Spirit, "Visit the minds of those who are *Yours*." What

---

[161] Ibid., I.43.3.
[162] St. Augustine, *On the Trinity* 6.10.11.
[163] CCC 1304; St. Thomas Aquinas, *Summa Theologiae* III.63.2, 3, 5; III.63.6, ad 2.

consoling words! What security and peace they inspire in us! We sing to the Holy Spirit, "I am *Yours*"! Surely, we belong to the Son as members of His own Mystical Body and to the Father as His own beloved sons and daughters in Jesus. In a unique way, however, we also *belong* to the Holy Spirit, the Father and Son's living Love and Beloved, who now dwells within us as the Beloved of *our* souls. Even more, what intimate peace fills us when, in prayer, we hear the Holy Spirit say to *us*, "You are Mine … and I am Yours." May the Holy Spirit Himself open our hearts to the unfathomable mystery of love conveyed in these precious words.

After Pentecost, the apostles lived always in the intimate presence of the Holy Spirit, their constant Companion and beloved Friend.[164] It was because they had become *intimate friends* of the Holy Spirit that the apostles were impelled to proclaim the risen Lord Jesus to the world. Through the sacrament of Confirmation, we share in this same wondrous blessing of Pentecost, the grace of an "intimate union" with the Holy Spirit, who dwells tenderly within us.[165] Through our intimacy with the Holy Spirit, we, too, are empowered and impelled to share the risen Lord with others.

We may have been very young or unaware of its profound meaning when we received Confirmation. Perhaps it is only now that we are beginning to realize what marvelous blessings have been lavished on us through this wondrous sacrament. It is never too late, however, for these magnificent graces lying dormant within us to bear fruit in our lives! At this very moment, let us ask the Holy Spirit to awaken and deepen within us the graces we have received at our Baptism and Confirmation,

---

[164] Concluding Prayer at Terce, Tuesday of Week II in Ordinary Time.
[165] CCC 1309.

regardless of our age or lack of understanding when we received these magnificent sacraments.

It is true that serious sin can destroy the life of grace within us until we repent and seek out the healing grace of the sacrament of Reconciliation. Nothing, however, can destroy the reality that through Baptism we are born again into the Family of the Trinity and that, through Confirmation, we forever belong in a special way to the Holy Spirit. If we have not yet received Baptism or Confirmation, let us join those preparing to receive these sacred mysteries, and, with all of our hearts say yes to the Trinity's infinite love and self-giving to us. If we already have received these beautiful sacraments, let us implore the Holy Spirit to enliven their graces within us and to make our lives new by His love.

The apostles' intimacy with the Holy Spirit empowered them to proclaim the risen Lord to the world. As the Word of the Lord spread, countless others became believers. These new Christians were drawn to the Lord not only by the apostles' anointed preaching but also and inseparably by the transformed lives of the apostles and disciples, who were wonderfully "filled with joy and the Holy Spirit" (Acts 13:52). May we, too, experience in our lives how tender and powerful is "the joy of the Holy Spirit."[166] Those who are transformed by intimate friendship with the Holy Spirit most surely become people of joy (Rom. 14:17). Others see this joy and want it. Let us pray that our own closeness with the Holy Spirit will allure many others to the Lord. Then may we hope to enter fully one day into the Trinity's heavenly bliss, drawn by the Holy Spirit, whose intimate love has been the secret of our joy here on earth.

[166] St. Bernard of Clairvaux, *Sermon Five on Diverse Topics*, Office of Readings, Twenty-Third Wednesday in Ordinary Time.

Select Bibliography

Ambrose of Milan, St. *On the Mysteries*. Translated by H. de Romestin, E. de Romestin, and H. T. F. Duckworth. Nicene and Post-Nicene Fathers, Second Series, vol. 10. Edited by Philip Schaff and Henry Wace. Buffalo, NY: Christian Literature, 1896. Revised and edited for New Advent by Kevin Knight. http://www.newadvent.org/ fathers/3405.htm.

Anaphora of St. John Chrysostom. Byzantine Catholic Archeparchy of Pittsburgh. https://mci.archpitt.org/liturgy/Divine_Liturgy_Anaphora_Chrysostom.html.

Angela of Foligno, St. *The Book of the Blessed Angela of Foligno: The Memorial*. In *Angela of Foligno: Complete Works*, 123–318. Translated by Paul Lachance, O.F.M. New York: Paulist Press, 1993.

Augustine of Hippo, St. *The Confessions*. Translated by J. G. Pilkington. Nicene and Post-Nicene Fathers, First Series, vol. 1. Edited by Philip Schaff. Buffalo, NY: Christian Literature, 1887. Revised and edited for New Advent by Kevin Knight. https://www.newadvent.org/fathers/1101.htm.

———. *Discourse on the Psalms, Ps. 32*, Office of Readings, feast of St. Cecilia. The Liturgy Archive. http://www.liturgies.net/ saints/cecilia/readings.htm.

———. Letter 130, to Proba. Translated by J. G. Cunningham. Nicene and Post-Nicene Fathers, First Series, vol. 1. Edited by Philip Schaff. Buffalo, NY: Christian Literature, 1887. Revised and edited for New Advent by Kevin Knight. https://www.newadvent.org/fathers/1102130.htm.

———. On the Trinity. Translated by Arthur West Haddan. Nicene and Post-Nicene Fathers, First Series, vol. 3. Edited by Philip Schaff. Buffalo, NY: Christian Literature, 1887. Revised and edited for New Advent by Kevin Knight. http://www.newadvent.org/fathers/1301.htm.

———. Sermon 34. Office of Readings, Tuesday of the Third Week of Easter. The Liturgy Archive. http://www.liturgies.net/Liturgies/Catholic/loh/easter/week3tuesdayor.htm.

———. Sermon 293. Office of Readings, feast of St. John the Baptist. St. John Church (Middletown, CT), June 23, 2012. https://stjohnct.wordpress.com/2012/06/23/solemnity-of-the-birth-of-john-the-baptist/.

Basil the Great, St. On the Holy Spirit. Translated by Blomfield Jackson. Nicene and Post-Nicene Fathers, Second Series, vol. 8. Edited by Philip Schaff and Henry Wace. Buffalo, NY: Christian Literature, 1895. Revised and edited for New Advent by Kevin Knight. https://www.newadvent.org/fathers/3202093.htm.

Bernard of Clairvaux. St. On the Song of Songs. Hymns and Chants. https://hymnsandchants.com/Texts/Sermons/SongOfSongs/SongOfSongs.htm.

———. Sermon Five on Diverse Topics. Office of Readings, Twenty-Third Wednesday in Ordinary Time. The Liturgy Archive. http://www.liturgies.net/Liturgies/Catholic/loh/week23wednesdayor.htm.

Bonaventure, St. *The Journey of the Mind to God*, 7.4. Office of Readings, feast of St. Bonaventure. The Liturgy Archive. http://www.liturgies.net/saints/bonaventure/readings.htm#loh.

Catechism of the Catholic Church. 2nd ed. Vatican: Libreria Editrice Vaticana, 2012. Vatican website. http://www.vatican.va/archive/ccc_css/archive/catechism/ccc_toc.htm.

Catherine of Siena. *The Dialogue*. Translated by Suzanne Noffke, O.P. New York: Paulist Press, 1980.

———. *The Letters of Catherine of Siena*. Vol. 2. Translated with introduction and notes by Suzanne Noffke, O.P. Tempe, AZ: Arizona Center for Medieval and Renaissance Studies, 2001.

Cyprian of Carthage. St. Treatise 4, *On the Lord's Prayer*. Translated by Robert Ernest Wallis. Ante-Nicene Fathers, vol. 5. Edited by Alexander Roberts, James Donaldson, and A. Cleveland Coxe. Buffalo, NY: Christian Literature, 1886. Revised and edited for New Advent by Kevin Knight. http://www.newadvent.org/fathers/050704.htm.

Cyril of Jerusalem, St. *Catechetical Lectures*. Translated by Edwin Hamilton Gifford. Nicene and Post-Nicene Fathers, Second Series, vol. 7. Edited by Philip Schaff and Henry Wace. Buffalo, NY: Christian Literature, 1894. Revised and edited for New Advent by Kevin Knight. http://www.newadvent.org/fathers/3101.htm.

———. *Catechetical Lecture 16*. Office of Readings, Monday of Easter Week Seven. The Liturgy Archive. http://www.liturgies.net/Liturgies/Catholic/loh/easter/week7mondayor.htm.

Francis de Sales, St. *Introduction to the Devout Life*. Grand Rapids, MI: Christian Classics Ethereal Library. https://ccel.org/ccel/d/desales/devout_life/cache/devout_life.pdf.

Gregory of Nyssa, St., *On "Not Three Gods."* Translated by H. A. Wilson. Nicene and Post-Nicene Fathers, Second Series, vol. 5. Edited by Philip Schaff and Henry Wace. Buffalo, NY: Christian Literature, 1893. Revised and edited for New Advent by Kevin Knight. https://www.newadvent.org/fathers/2905.htm.

———. *On the Holy Spirit, Against the Macedonians*. Translated by William Moore and Henry Austin Wilson. Nicene and Post-Nicene Fathers, Second Series, vol. 5. Edited by Philip Schaff and Henry Wace. Buffalo, NY: Christian Literature, 1893. Revised and edited for New Advent by Kevin Knight. https://www.newadvent.org/fathers/2903.htm.

———. Homily 3 on the Lord's Prayer: *Hallowed Be Thy Name, Thy Kingdom Come*. Translated by Theodore G. Stylianopoulos, 2003. Orthodox Prayer. https://www.orthodoxprayer.org/Articles_files/GregoryNyssa-Homily3%20Lords%20Prayer.html.

Grignion de Montfort, Louis-Marie, St. *True Devotion to the Blessed Virgin*. http://www.montfortian.info/writings/files/The-True-Devotion-to-Mary.pdf.

International Commission on English in the Liturgy. *Pastoral Care of the Sick: Rites of Anointing and Viaticum*. General Introduction. https://www.saginaw.org/sites/default/files/2018-01/Pastoral_Care_of_the_Sick.pdf.

Irenaeus, St. *Against Heresies*. Translated by Alexander Roberts and William Rambaut. Ante-Nicene Fathers, vol. 1. Edited by Alexander Roberts, James Donaldson, and A. Cleveland Coxe. Buffalo, NY: Christian Literature, 1885. Revised and edited for New Advent by Kevin Knight. http://www.newadvent.org/fathers/0103.htm.

John Chrysostom, St. *Baptismal Instructions*. Translated and Annotated by Paul W. Harkins. Volume 31 of Ancient Christian Writers, The Works of the Fathers in Translation. Edited by

Johannes Quasten and Walter J. Burghardt, S.J. New York: Newman Press, 1963.

John of the Cross, St. *Living Flame of Love*. In *The Collected Works of St. John of the Cross*. Translated by Kieran Kavanaugh, O.C.D., and Otilio Rodriguez, O.C.D. Intro. Kieran Kavanaugh. Washington, DC: ICS Publications, 1973.

———. *The Spiritual Canticle*. In *The Collected Works of St. John of the Cross*. Translated by Kieran Kavanaugh, O.C.D., and Otilio Rodriguez, O.C.D. Intro. Kieran Kavanaugh. Washington, DC: ICS Publications, 1973.

John Paul II, Pope St. Apostolic Letter on the Christian Meaning of Human Suffering *Salvifici Doloris* (February 11, 1984).

John XXIII, Pope St. Apostolic Constitution Convoking Vatican Council II *Humanae Salutis* (Of Human Salvation) (December 25, 1961).

Kavanagh, Aidan. *The Shape of Baptism: The Rite of Christian Initiation*. New York: Pueblo, 1978.

Leo XIII, Pope. Encyclical Letter on the Holy Spirit *Divinum Illud Munus* (May 9, 1897).

Martinez, Luis. *True Devotion to the Holy Spirit*. Translated by Sr. M. Aquinas. Manchester, New Hampshire: Sophia Institute Press, 2000.

Newman, John Henry, St. *Meditations and Devotions*. London: Longmans, Green, 1916. https://archive.org/details/TheWorks OfCardinalNewmanMeditations.

———. "Sermon 19: The Indwelling Spirit." In *Plain and Parochial Sermons*. Vol. 2. London: Longmans, Green, 1908. https://newmanreader.org/works/parochial/volume2/sermon19.html.

Paul VI, Pope St. Apostolic Constitution on the Sacrament of Confirmation *Divinae Consortium Naturae* (August 15, 1971).

https://archive.org/details/paulvisapostolic00cath/page/7/mode/2up.

Peter Damian, St. *Life of St. Romuald*. Office of Readings, feast of St. Romuald. The Liturgy Archive. http://www.liturgies.net/saints/romuald/readings.htm#loh.

Raymond of Capua. *The Life of Catherine of Siena*. Translated, introduced, and annotated by Conleth Kearns, O.P. Wilmington, DE: Michael Glazier, 1980.

Rite of Penance. Liturgy Office, England and Wales. https://www.liturgyoffice.org.uk/Resources/Penance/Penance-Intro.pdf.

Second Vatican Council. Constitution on the Sacred Liturgy *Sacrosanctum Concilium* (December 4, 1963).

Seton, Elizabeth Bayley, St. *Correspondence and Journals 1793–1808*. In *Collected Writings*, volume 1, edited by Regina Bechtle, S.C., and Judith Metz, S.C. Hyde Park, NY: New City Press, 2000. Vincentian Heritage Collections at Via Sapientiae. https://via.library.depaul.edu/cgi/viewcontent.cgi?article=1008&context=vincentian_ebooks.

———. *Correspondence and Journals 1808–1820*. In *Collected Writings*, volume 2, edited by Regina Bechtle, S.C., and Judith Metz, S.C. Hyde Park, NY: New City Press, 2002. Vincentian Heritage Collections at Via Sapientiae. https://via.library.depaul.edu/cgi/viewcontent.cgi?article=1010&context=vincentian_ebooks.

Thomas Aquinas, St. *Commentary on the Gospel of John*. Part II: Chapters 8–21. Translated by Fabian R. Larcher, O.P. Albany, NY: Magi Books, 1998. https://isidore.co/aquinas/english/SSJohn.htm.

———. *Commentary on Psalm 46*. Translated by Steven Loughlin. De Sales University Aquinas Translation Project. http://hosted.desales.edu/w4/philtheo/loughlin/ATP/.

————. *Sermon for the Feast of Pentecost.* Published as "Aquinas's Sermon for the Feast of Pentecost: A Rare Glimpse of Thomas the Preaching Friar." Translated by Peter Kwasniewski and Jeremy Holmes from the provisional critical edition of the Leonine Commission. https://isidore.co/aquinas/Serm11Emitte.htm#text.

————. *Summa Contra Gentiles.* Book IV: Salvation. Translated by Charles J. O'Neil. New York: Hanover House, 1957. https://isidore.co/aquinas/english/ContraGentiles.htm.

————. *Summa Theologiae.* 2nd rev. ed. 1920. Translated by Fathers of the English Dominican Province. Online Edition by Kevin Knight, 2017. New Advent. https://www.newadvent.org/summa/.

Vianney, John. St. *Instructions on the Catechism.* Crossroads Initiative. https://www.crossroadsinitiative.com/media/articles/catechetical-instructions/.

Index of Scriptural Citations

Index of Scriptural Citations

Index of Names and Subjects

About the Author

Sr. Mary Ann Fatula, O.P., Ph.D., served as a professor of theology at Ohio Dominican University and for more than thirty years taught theology there. Sr. Mary Ann is the author of *Catherine of Siena's Way*, *The Holy Spirit: Unbounded Gift of Joy*, and *Thomas Aquinas, Preacher and Friend*. Her most recent book is *Heaven's Splendor*, published by Sophia Institute Press.

Sophia Institute

Sophia Institute is a nonprofit institution that seeks to nurture the spiritual, moral, and cultural life of souls and to spread the gospel of Christ in conformity with the authentic teachings of the Roman Catholic Church.

Sophia Institute Press fulfills this mission by offering translations, reprints, and new publications that afford readers a rich source of the enduring wisdom of mankind.

Sophia Institute also operates the popular online resource CatholicExchange.com. *Catholic Exchange* provides world news from a Catholic perspective as well as daily devotionals and articles that will help readers to grow in holiness and live a life consistent with the teachings of the Church.

In 2013, Sophia Institute launched Sophia Institute for Teachers to renew and rebuild Catholic culture through service to Catholic education. With the goal of nurturing the spiritual, moral, and cultural life of souls, and an abiding respect for the role and work of teachers, we strive to provide materials and programs that are at once enlightening to the mind and ennobling to the heart; faithful and complete, as well as useful and practical.

Sophia Institute gratefully recognizes the Solidarity Association for preserving and encouraging the growth of our apostolate over the course of many years. Without their generous and timely support, this book would not be in your hands.

www.SophiaInstitute.com
www.CatholicExchange.com
www.SophiaInstituteforTeachers.org

Sophia Institute Press® is a registered trademark of Sophia Institute.
Sophia Institute is a tax-exempt institution as defined by the
Internal Revenue Code, Section 501(c)(3). Tax ID 22-2548708.